London

at its best

BY ROBERT S. KANE

The World at Its Best Travel Series
BRITAIN AT ITS BEST
FRANCE AT ITS BEST
SPAIN AT ITS BEST
GERMANY AT ITS BEST
ITALY AT ITS BEST
HAWAII AT ITS BEST
LONDON AT ITS BEST
PARIS AT ITS BEST

A to Z World Travel Guides
GRAND TOUR A TO Z: THE CAPITALS OF EUROPE
EASTERN EUROPE A TO Z
SOUTH PACIFIC A TO Z
CANADA A TO Z
ASIA A TO Z
SOUTH AMERICA A TO Z
AFRICA A TO Z

Robert S. Kane

London
at its best

 **PASSPORT BOOKS**

Trade Imprint of National Textbook Company
Lincolnwood, Illinois U.S.A.

For Michael Ross

map by palacios

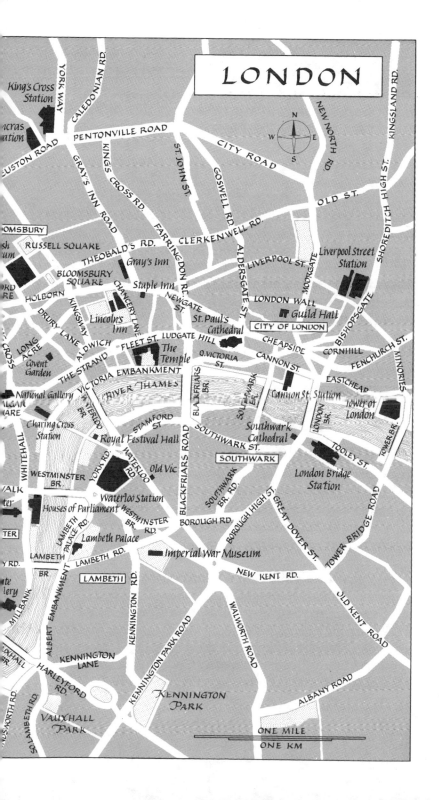

Contents

Foreword
Everybody's Favorite City

London has it made. By that, I mean it has no image problem. It's Everybody's Favorite City: Continental Europeans from the south, Scandinavians from the east, the most nationalist of Scots from the north, and Welshmen and Irishmen from the west, former colonials from every corner of the globe who are Commonwealth citizens and never need go near the place if they don't choose to. And ourselves—the country cousins from across the water. We have always been pushovers for London.

Which is not at all a bad thing. Neither for us nor, for that matter, for London. It is just that we are not always sure why it is we are so partial to this oft-damp town tucked into the interior of a northern island detached from the continent of Europe. There are those among us who like it not for the wrong reasons, but for not enough valid reasons. The visitor's London is too often a limited London. We put up at a nice hotel, take in the Abbey and St. Paul's and maybe the National Gallery and a section or two of the vast British Museum.

We watch the guard change at Buckingham Palace *and* at the Horse Guards (priding ourselves on being inordinately thorough in the realm of spit-and-polish). And damned if we don't have tea at Fortnum's fountain and perhaps a chophouse dinner. London is cashmere sweaters, a bit of Wedgwood or Royal Derby, and more theater than we take in for the rest of the year—and then some—back home. Upon our return, all that changes are the titles of the plays. We're back at Harrods and Burberrys and the Bond Street boutiques, and we may go as far afield as the Impressionists at the Courtauld in Bloomsbury or the State Apartments in Windsor Castle.

My point is that there is so very much more that is so very accessible. In no major city of the planet is veering from the beaten path—and believe me, I am all for the beaten path for starters—more pleasurable or more rewarding. *London at Its Best* is not unlike the companion volumes in this series, in that its author is unabashedly subjective on a number of counts. The most important are what is included and what is not. I devote a lot of space to things to see and places to go. I am not now and never have been of the school that discourages popping into museums and historic churches and landmark houses on the shockingly specious grounds that if you've seen one, you have seen the lot.

At the same time, I have worked hard at researching creature comforts. As with my other *World at Its Best* guides, this one presents a substantial quantity of personally evaluated hotels—categorized by me as *Luxury, First Class,* and *Moderate*—that I have either lived in, eaten and drunk at, or quite thoroughly inspected; and of a wide gamut of restaurants—again in three price ranges—from simple-snack to quite splendid, with the majority in the middle category and with varying types of cuisines, as well. There's a section on atmospheric pubs, for both solid and liquid nourishment, and a chapter on London To Watch—legitimate theaters, opera, ballet, and concerts.

I begin at the beginning, with a bit of background—enough, I hope, to whet the newcomer's appetite—a brief summary of what has gone before in the couple of millennia since the Romans came north and transformed the Celts' *Lyndin* into the Latin *Londinium*. Then comes the nitty-gritty: from a geographic orientation, through my own dozen-plus London requisite destinations, into the various layers of London as I see them—its architecture (an alphabetical sampler from the Bank of England to the University of London), churches (by Wren and Gibbs and by earlier Gothic and later Victorian architects, as well), museums (reports on what I consider the couple of dozen most visitworthy), the too-often underappreciated parks and squares, and the periphery (this last embraces visits to easy-to-reach, treasure-filled, stately homes not far from town).

A selection of what I consider to be the ten best day-long excursions in the countryside follows—from Bath in the west to Canterbury in the east, from Cambridge in the north to Salisbury in the south. There is a chapter on shops that I've scouted, divided alphabetically into a score of categories, not excluding all of the major department stores and the street markets that are unique to London.

Well, then, I've given you an idea of how I look at London and how I—presumptuous foreigner that I am—attempt to interpret it from, say, Sir Christopher Wren (there's a biographical sketch in Chapter 2 of this building genius who never trained as an architect) to newspapers and magazines (they're appraised in Chapter 7). What I write least about are the Londoners themselves. They are there, along with their city and its institutions, for each of us to get to know on his or her own terms. They do not always profess to understand our fascination with their town. But they invariably welcome us sincerely and, often, wittily. Coupled with the setting for this kind of hospitality, we have no right, as their guests, to ask any more.

ROBERT S. KANE

London To Know

BACKGROUND BRIEFING

It may well be that London has always tried harder because it is an island city, physically detached from the larger Continent, and anxious to prove that the English Channel and the North and Irish seas were quite the reverse of barriers to its development. Your Londoner today is neither aggressive nor restless nor impatient. But surely his forebears must have been. Else how would such a great and beautiful and, for long, powerful city have evolved on a dampish, northern island?

Not that London was without certain advantages. A head start for one. And a name that stuck, for another. The Celts (poets then, as now) were calling the place *Lyndin*—a name with a nice ring to it that meant waterside fortress—as long ago as the first century of the Christian era, when the Roman legions happened up from France to settle in. Always better at adapting than originating, they simply Latinized Lyndin to *Londinium*.

There was a brief period, not long after their arrival, when it was touch and go whether they could stay. The Celts' own queen, Boadicea, by name, tried to oust the rascals from the fort they had built. But to no avail. Roman walls went up, and Roman laws were introduced. The Roman culture and the Latin language—all had been implanted by the time of the Roman exodus 400 years later.

There followed that confusing, albeit alliterative, run of the "E" kings—Egbert and Ethelwulf and Ethelbald and Ethelbert and Ethelred and Edmund and Edred and Edwy and Edgar. Until Alfred the Great—no one has explained his refreshingly distinctive name—none of the Kings was especially London-oriented. Alfred changed all this. He chose London as his capital, which was an achievement in itself. But he was, as well, a pursuer of peace in an age when war was the norm.

Additionally, he set his people's sights on education and literacy, first setting up a school for his largely illiterate nobles and, second, ordering translated the handful of important books of the time from Latin—still the literary tongue of his realm—into English. After settling in, he gave London its first proper government.

WILLIAM THE CONQUEROR'S LONDON

London then was the easterly sector of what all these subsequent centuries has been called the City—which continues jealously to guard its independence of the rest of London. Its government was such that with the invasion of England by William the Conqueror in 1066 the City of London was treated separately, allowing its citizens to elect their officials democratically, as they had since Alfred's time. The Tower of London—or at least the White Tower, its nucleus—went up during William's reign.

But just before then, William's predecessor and boyhood chum, the sainted Edward the Confessor, had begun personally to supervise the building of Westminster Abbey to replace an earlier church that had been on the site. It was Edward, with his attention to the Abbey at Westminster, who succeeded in transferring the Court and government from the Tower area of the City to Westminster—where it has remained for almost a millennium, with hardly a break.

All the while, under later kings like Richard I (who gave the City the Lord Mayor and the corporation form of government it has never abandoned) and Henry III (who built still another Westminster Abbey—the one we know today), London continued to expand, economically, as well as architecturally and politically. In medieval centuries, craft and trade guilds became important. Lawyers formed their still-extant—and still eminently visitable—Inns of Court.

THE TUDORS AND THE REFORMATION

At midpoint in the mid-fifteenth century, England had spent a hundred fruitless years fighting to retain her French territory, to no avail. The ugly civil strife with the beautiful name—Wars of the Roses, between Yorks and Lancasters—followed, with Henry VII's victory at Bosworth Field and then the eventful reign of his son, Henry VIII. Political turmoil, war, disease—nothing stopped London's growth. Although Holbein and other painters had to be imported from the Continent, there was no dearth of domestic architects or artisans.

Henry VIII's reign saw Hampton Court erected as but one of many Tudor-style forerunners of later Renaissance buildings. It was Henry VIII, of course, whose complex marital situation led to the break with the Roman Catholic Church and the establishment of the Church of England. The religious schism resulting was to trouble England for many successive reigns.

Three of Henry's half-dozen wives bore him children,

and each reigned: the bright but sickly youngster, Edward
VI, for half a decade; the bitterly unhappy Bloody Mary,
for still another half-decade, which was marked by her
disastrous marriage to Catholic Spain's Philip II and a
wholesale massacre of Protestant subjects thereafter; and
then Elizabeth I—the spinster Elizabeth, during whose 45
years on the throne England became a world power to be
reckoned with. Elizabeth resumed the Protestantism of
her father over the Catholicism of her half-sister.
Elizabeth's fleet defeated the great Spanish Armada of her
ex-brother-in-law and spurned suitor, Philip II. Elizabeth's knights—Raleigh was, of course, but one—secured
the colonial empire of the New World.

STUARTS TO THE THRONE

It was Elizabeth's reign that produced Shakespeare,
Marlowe, Spenser, Bacon, and Drake. The Renaissance architecture of these years took its name from the Queen:
These were the decades of the great Elizabethan country
houses like Knole; of sprouting new colleges at both Oxford and Cambridge; of elaborate formal gardens setting
off the manors and palaces; and of design that formed the
basis of the succeeding reign. Jacobean—named for James
I—is best typified by Hatfield House, the manor that went
up on the grounds of an earlier, smaller house where
Elizabeth succeeded to the throne; it was followed by the
Renaissance style of the remarkable Inigo Jones.

The son of the ill-fated Mary Queen of Scots (whom
Elizabeth imprisoned and beheaded), already James VI of
Scotland, succeeded Elizabeth as James I of England, the
first of the Stuart dynasty. We know him best for his still-
used version of the Bible. He ushered in a troubled era.
Charles I, his successor, was so disliked by Parliament that
it tried him for high treason and then chopped his head

off. (You may see a statue of him in Whitehall, not far from where he was beheaded.) The bleak, stern Commonwealth of the Cromwells, father Oliver and son Richard, followed—but only for a decade. Charles II (in the company of orange-vending Nell Gwynn, perhaps the most celebrated of his mistresses) effected the spirited Restoration—not as lavish, perhaps, as the contemporary France of Louis XIV, but one that put London in high spirits, completely unprepared for the tragedy of the plague that killed off a third of its citizens, only to be cruelly followed by the Great Fire that razed the whole of the City. A young inventor and astronomer—not trained as an architect—named Sir Christopher Wren, designed a new St. Paul's Cathedral as a memorial to the old one claimed by the Great Fire. A prolific, long-lived genius, Wren designed 150-plus churches, inspiring an entire school of followers, who created much of the London of ensuing decades.

QUEEN ANNE AND THE FOUR GEORGES

The Catholic-Protestant confusion engendered by Henry VIII continued, even now, to influence the choice of occupants for the throne, to the point where Catholic James II was booted out, and Protestant Dutchman Prince William of Orange was called across the North Sea to reign with his English wife, Mary, one of the two Protestant daughters of the deposed James II. The second daughter, Anne, followed William and Mary to the throne and had more success in giving her name to the handsome Baroque school of furniture and design that sprouted over England than in giving birth to an heir—or even heiress. Poor Anne, who reigned only a dozen years, was pregnant 17 times by her rather simple, albeit good-natured, Danish husband, but only one child lived, to die young, at the age of 11.

Anne, like her predecessors, William and Mary, lived

away from the center of town, mainly in the palace at Kensington, the state rooms of which are today open to the public. She never visited Scotland as Queen, although the significant Act of Union between England and Scotland came about during her reign.

German relatives—the easy-to-remember four Georges —succeeded Anne. Of these, only the last two were especially interesting: long-reigning George III, who, because of his repressive policies, lost England its non-Canadian colonies in North America; and George IV, because, while Prince Regent during his father's latterly insane years, he commissioned a genius named John Nash to build what we now term Regency London. What Wren did for Baroque London, Nash did for the capital of the early nineteenth century, with Regent's Park, Regent Street, Waterloo Place, and Carlton House Terrace. (Alas, "Prinny's" Carlton House—his town palace—is no more.)

The city had not, to be sure, stagnated during the eighteenth century, which saw the construction of Grosvenor, Hanover, Bedford, and Soho squares and which was, after all, the great era of Georgian architecture and applied arts ranging from silver to furniture. Inigo Jones (whose Whitehall Banqueting House is a requisite London destination) introduced the neoclassic Palladian into London from Italy, and Robert Adam later became its chief practitioner. Cabinetmakers with immortal names like Chippendale, Sheraton, Hepplewhite, and the multitalented William Kent created furniture for Georgian houses. Slender-spired colonnaded churches—James Gibbs's St. Martin-in-the-Fields in London's Trafalgar Square is a prime example—went up in profusion. And the style found great favor in the American colonies, where we still often refer to Georgian houses and churches—as well as latter-day adaptations like banks and schools—as "colonial."

English painters came into their own—late, if contrasted

with the Continent, but great: William Hogarth, Sir Joshua Reynolds, Sir Thomas Lawrence, and those other painters of beautiful English ladies and beautiful English landscapes, namely, Thomas Gainsborough and George Romney, not to mention Scots Sir Henry Raeburn and Allan Ramsay.

VICTORIAN EXPANSION

Victoria, a niece of the brothers George IV and William IV and a granddaughter of George III, ascended the throne in 1837 and stayed there—much of the time in mourning at Windsor for Albert, her creative and talented German-born husband who died in 1861—until 1901. Her reign of 64 years was the longest in English history and saw England evolve into a democratic nation during a long, mostly peaceful era. Victorian London is to be seen at every turn—the City is full of the heavily proportioned construction of the era, with its penchant for the neo-Gothic.

But so much else bears the name of that long-reigning lady: furniture, interiors, fiction, and, hardly the least, morals. This was the age when Britain consolidated its far-flung empire, and even the late twentieth-century traveler is not allowed to forget it; my atlas lists nearly three-score Victorias around the world, ranging from the capital of British Columbia to a fjord in Greenland.

Victoria reigned for so long that her portly heir, Edward VII, was sixty when he succeeded, along with his breath-takingly beautiful—albeit hard-of-hearing—queen, Alexandra, daughter of Denmark's King Christian IX. His reign was short—just under a decade—but still it constituted an era, and not as giddy an era as we have been led to believe. Edward VII rarely gets the credit he deserves for diplomatic talents. He was intelligent, and his tact and brains had a

lot to do with development of the cordial Anglo-French relations that were to prove so valuable in World War I.

Britain emerged a victor from that conflict, and the decades before World War II saw—among a lot else—the very
proper reign of George V and the formidable Queen Mary,
as well as the first Labour government under Ramsay
MacDonald and the abdication that the world has never
stopped talking about: that of the globally popular, brand-
new-to-the-throne Edward VIII, who became Duke of
Windsor and the husband of a twice-divorced American,
Wallis Warfield Simpson, who died on April 23, 1986, in
Paris and was buried next to the Duke.

NAZI BOMBS—AND TODAY'S BRITAIN

World War II was Britain's darkest, yet bravest, hour. Following Nazi Germany's invasion of Poland in 1939, Britain entered the war. The coalition government of Winston
Churchill led it to victory; although after the invasion and
occupation of France in 1940, it fought alone, until joined
by the United States at the end of 1941. London—and
other areas of the country—suffered from repeated World
War II bombings. Great portions of it were blitzed, and
many of its people were killed or wounded. No people
were braver than Londoners during World War II, and at
no other time have the British and American peoples been
closer than during World War II and the immediate post-
World War II years. Chances are that the Underground
platform at which you wait for a train was slept upon by
countless Londoners in the course of almost nightly air
raids.

The well-liked wartime king, George VI, was a postwar
casualty. He died in 1952, and his elder daughter, Princess
Elizabeth (born 1926), became Queen Elizabeth II, while
animal-viewing in the bush lodge called Treetops during

an official visit to Kenya. (You read a bronze plaque to that effect on the Treetops terrace.) Elizabeth and her husband, Prince Philip, Duke of Edinburgh—a former Greek prince and nephew of the late Lord Mountbatten, last British viceroy of India—have four children: Princes Edward (born 1964) and Andrew (born 1960), Princess Anne (born 1950), and the eldest and heir apparent, Charles, Prince of Wales (born 1948), married in 1981 to the former Lady Diana Spencer.

Following the Royal Family on the social scale is the hereditary peerage, embracing (along with their families, many of whose members have lesser titles) 26 dukes, 200 earls, nearly 500 barons, 132 viscounts, and large numbers of baronets, who are addressed as "Sir," as also are knights, who are granted their titles only for their own lifetimes in recognition of distinctive services of one sort or another to the nation. Knights are only a part of the nearly 700 Honors Lists recipients designated annually by the government and ranging from titled lifetime (nonhereditary) barons to recipients of the Order of the British Empire and Companion of the British Empire, who are identified by initials following their names (O.B.E., C.B.E.) rather than titles preceding them. Additionally, there are honors bestowed by the sovereign acting without the advice of the government. These include the Knights of the Garter, the Thistle (for Scots), and the coveted, rarely bestowed Order of Merit.

CONTEMPORARY LONDON

London's oldest and most historic sector, the earlier-described City area, has been self-governing, with its own Lord Mayor and Corporation, since it was founded in medieval times. The Lord Mayor is aided in governing by a couple of dozen additional aldermen, 159 councilmen, and a pair of sheriffs—all of whom work with the guilds, or livery companies, whose origins go back more than half a millennium. Out of more than 80 guilds, a favored dozen are officially designated "great"; they carry considerable prestige and include the Mercers', Grocers', Drapers', Fishmongers', Goldsmiths', and Haberdashers'.

The one-square-mile-in-area City, which continues to run its own police department (its bobbies have distinctive red-and-white sleeve insignia), is not unlike New York's Wall Street area in that it is virtually deserted by night, with but a few thousand residents, in contrast to the half-million-plus who labor in the area by day—many of them eternally dressed in the traditional dark-suit "uniforms," topped by the derby hats that are known as bowlers in England, and never, ever without tightly rolled umbrellas.

The rest of London is something else again. Its oldest sector is Westminster, the area that developed around the Abbey and that took its name because of its position west of the City. By the late nineteenth century, the London area was a confusing complex of political entities, and in 1888 the lot joined forces as the County of London, to be governed by the London County Council.

Much more recently, in 1965, Greater London came into being, with an area of 620 square miles, extending beyond the old County of London into several surrounding counties, with a population close to eight million and under the aegis of the Greater London Council until 1986, when the council—which operated from County Hall, a massive 1920s block on the north bank of the Thames—was abolished, and its functions dispersed among other governmental bodies.

If Britain has come full circle in this second Elizabethan era, so has its capital. It was during the reign of the first Elizabeth that the Empire became great, with London assuming international dominance, both commercial and political. It has been during the reign of the second Elizabeth that the Empire has been largely dismantled. The overwhelming majority of the colonies around the world—the invincible Empire on which the sun never set—are now mostly sovereign republics voluntarily associated with the Commonwealth of Nations. Commonwealth countries range from more than 30 old-timers like Australia and Canada to relative newcomers like Tonga and the Bahamas. Most are republics; some remain monarchies governed by their own prime ministers but with Queen Elizabeth II doubling as their head of state, as well as head of state of the United Kingdom.

Regardless of the nature of the association of their governments with Whitehall and the Crown, London remains a formidable lure to substantial segments of the population of every Commonwealth country, just as English remains the *lingua franca* of each—varied nationalist linguistic sentiments notwithstanding. If the Commonwealth helped make London one of the most cosmopolitan of capitals, then the Continent will make it even more so. For within decades of the loss of the Empire came membership in the European Common Market. Of course, there will always be an England—and there will always be a London as its capital.

2

London To See

LAY OF THE LAND

The beauty of London comes through the window of one's sedate black taxi, from the moment of arrival: the campanile of Big Ben and the tower of Parliament over the Thames, Victorian grandeur and Georgian elegance, Regency terraces and Renaissance palaces. A further glance or two reveals the polished brass of Mayfair and its glossy shops, churches by Wren and Gibbs and the cathedrals, department stores unsurpassed in style or luxury by those of any city, pageantry that is positively medieval in its splendor, bus conductors who are earthily Cockney, warmly Caribbean, sedately East Indian. What primarily interests most visitors is the West End and the City, contiguous areas on the north side of the Thames.

Start in Piccadilly Circus, core of the visitor's West End. Almost due north is Regent Street, with its great stores. Almost due east is Shaftesbury Avenue, worth remembering because it leads to the maze of legitimate theaters that are a prime London lure and to the foreign-cuisine restaurants of Soho.

Walk south on an extension of Regent Street or on Haymarket, running parallel, and you are in the ancient St. James's area. First major cross street is club-lined Pall Mall, and one walks east on it to Trafalgar Square, continuing east to the Strand. In just a few blocks, it changes its name to Fleet Street, at once newspaper center of the country and the beginning of the original, still separately governed City. The Strand is as good a place as any to cross one of the many bridges leading over the Thames to South London; Waterloo Bridge leads to Royal Festival Hall. Farther east, the crossing could be made on London Bridge, with Southwark Cathedral just over the water.

Return now to where we started, Piccadilly Circus. Walk directly west on Piccadilly. Within a few blocks, just beyond the Royal Academy of Arts, is fashionable Bond Street. You may walk it due north until you come to the major intersecting artery, Oxford Street—with department stores, including the giant Selfridges.

Return now to Piccadilly, and continue walking west. On your left is Green Park. Contiguous with it are Buckingham Palace Gardens and St. James's Park. Most impressive approach to Buckingham Palace is The Mall, cutting through St. James's and Green parks and passing a cluster of royal or once-royal residences—St. James's Palace, Marlborough House, Clarence House, and Lancaster House.

Return once again to Piccadilly, walking it until it terminates at Park Lane. Turn right onto Park Lane, following it to the north, alongside Hyde Park into Mayfair, whose maze of charming streets provides the stuff of limitless exploration. Still another park, Regent's, is way to the north of Mayfair. Kensington, where many visitors stay, lies southwest of Hyde Park. Knightsbridge, Belgravia, and Chelsea—all fashionable—border the park, stretching to Cheyne Walk and the Chelsea Embankment on the Thames.

If London is not quite as street-sign-compulsive as Paris, it is way, way ahead of New York and of such Continental cities as Rome. And the signs invariably tell you not only the name of the street, but the name of the borough and its directional (W. 1, S.W. 2) designation

THE ESSENTIAL LONDON: A BAKER'S DOZEN REQUISITES

National Portrait Gallery (St. Martin's Lane): I often wish that my first destination on my first trip to London had been the National Portrait Gallery. Its concept is such a brilliant one that the Scots have adapted it in Edinburgh, and they do not often emulate their English cousins so obviously. The purpose is to give one an idea of what Britain has been all about, these many centuries, by means of portraits of its leading personalities—not only kings, queens, and royal mistresses, as important as they have been, heaven knows, but politicians, writers, poets, scientists, and musicians. You'll find the works of such painters as Sir Peter Lely and Sir Godfrey Kneller—the German-born portraitist who rose to eminence in Charles II's court—and of later English masters like Reynolds, Romney, and Lawrence, and of many foreign painters, too. A museum folder "intended for the visitor with only a limited period of time at his disposal" suggests viewing these "Six Famous Portraits in Fifteen Minutes": Sir Walter Raleigh by Nicholas Hilliard; Queen Elizabeth I by Gheeraerts the Younger; Henry VIII by—of course, you know—Holbein; Shakespeare by an unknown artist; that superbly gossipy Restoration diarist, Samuel Pepys, by John Hayls; and the remarkably talented Brontë sisters—Charlotte, Emily, and Anne—by their brother, Branwell. Gets you in the mood, sets the stage; that's what the National Portrait Gallery does. And very well, indeed.

Tower of London (Tower Hill): If the Tower, to use the vernacular, is not quite where it's all at, it surely is where it all began. William the Conqueror founded it a millennium ago, and succeeding sovereigns took up where he left off. The Tower has served as military citadel, royal residence, political prison, mint, observatory, and repository of royal property ranging from precious documents to crown jewels. Even today the Tower remains, nominally at least, a royal palace under the direct control of the sovereign.

Its Governor has the privilege of calling home the Queen's House, a Tudor mansion in the Tower complex. Troops under the Governor's command are the yeoman warders. Their usual blue uniform is relatively somber, but they are best known (thanks in modern times to a gin called Beefeater) by brilliant red, black, and gold outfits, with Elizabethan white ruffs around their necks, that were designed in the sixteenth century. They are all mature men, for to become a yeoman warder one must have been not only a sergeant in one of the military services, but a recipient of the Good Conduct or Long Service medal, as well.

Major building is the White Tower, so called because it was originally whitewashed. It was home to a long line of medieval kings; they lived on the top floor, conducted business in the council chamber just below, and worshiped in the beautiful St. John the Evangelist Chapel.

See the aptly named Bloody Tower—for it was where the ghoulish sixteenth-century royal murders occurred. Either Richard III or Henry VII was the culprit, depending on which version of history one goes along with; victims were the young princes, Edward V and the Duke of York. The Crown Jewels repose in the contemporary, subsurface Jewel House. They comprise a dazzling assortment of orbs, scepters, swords, and, of course, crowns, with the range from Edward the Confessor to Queen Mother Elizabeth— or, in other words, about a thousand years. There remains the Chapel Royal of St. Peter ad Vincula, a Tudor treasure, at whose Sunday morning services the public is welcome.

Westminster Abbey (Victoria Street)—or the Minster in the west, as contrasted to St. Paul's and the Tower in the City to the east—is the core of the "new" London, the area that the court, government, and church developed at the time of Edward the Confessor, a thousand years ago. The Abbey is peculiar in that it is not actually an abbey (monks have not been resident since the time of the first of the three structures on the site), and it is not a cathedral (for it is not the seat, or *cathedra*, of the bishop of a diocese).

It is, instead, designated a "royal particular," and it has become, over the centuries, a national history book in a Gothic cover. It goes back to the mid-thirteenth century, and its elongated, splendidly high nave—despite the jarring presence of inappropriate crystal chandeliers that illuminate it and an early Victorian choir screen—is among the handsomest in England. So, for that matter, is the choir, even though much of it is surprisingly modern. There are fine tombs—Eleanor of Castile's is a standout—and there are other corners and vistas that are esthetically, as well as spiritually, moving. Monarch after monarch (including Elizabeth I and her adversary, Mary Queen of Scots) is buried within, and so are poets and politicians and war heroes, there being a chapel dedicated to Royal Air Force men killed in the World War II Battle of Britain. The fan vaulting of Henry VII's chapel is superb. (It would be even more so without the distracting multicolored flags protruding from its walls.)

But withal, the Abbey comes through, to at least one not infrequent visitor, as too well scrubbed, too classroomy, too official. (And, in recent years, too commercial. One may visit the nave and cloisters without charge, but a ticket must be purchased for other areas.) I prefer Southwark, across the river, or a Wren—or pre-Fire—church in the City. But you must make a duty call at the Abbey; after all, every sovereign has been crowned there—on the Coronation Chair enclosing the ancient Stone of Scone—since Edward the Confessor, save two: Edward V, the boy king who was murdered in the Tower in 1483, aged 13, and Edward VIII, who abdicated before his coronation.

Houses of Parliament (Parliament Square) are mostly—there are significant exceptions—Victorian, and aside from their importance as the seat of the national legislature (a legislature that once controlled the destiny of great chunks of the world's territory), they represent, at least to me, Victorian architecture and interior design at their most sublime. Westminster—or, more officially, the Palace of Westminster—is everything that the Parliament of a great nation should be: awesome, elegant, monumentally proportioned, and splendidly sited on the Thames.

Its oldest component part, Westminster Hall, goes back to the eleventh century. With its beamed Gothic ceiling, the hall still sees service as a conference site and as the place where monarchs and national heroes lie in state before burial. St. Stephen's Hall is early Victorian, a replica of the ancient structure that served as the House of Commons for several event-packed centuries. The adjoining sixteenth-century cloister with its fan vaulting is visitworthy.

Parliament proper takes its bearings from the elaborate Central Lobby: Commons is in one direction; Lords, in the other. There are galleries in both houses for visitors; Britons get tickets through their MPs; foreigners mostly take their chances by waiting in line out in front the day they want to get in.

The House of Lords has less power than its opposite number, but its quarters are infinitely more attractive. This, after all, is where the sovereign addresses both of the houses at the Opening of Parliament; thus, the splendid throne and adjacent Robing Room. Commons is simpler for two reasons. First is that traditionally the sovereign has never been welcome within its precincts. Second is that it was bombed out during World War II and had to be rebuilt. The result is a chamber done on traditional lines but with near barnlike severity. Worth noting: Members' benches in Lords are upholstered in red; those in Commons, in green. Colors of benches in the upper and lower houses of Parliaments throughout the Commonwealth are identical in color, almost without exception.

British Museum/British Library (Great Russell Street) is the most marvelous of the catchall museums, abounding in treasures from every corner of what had been the world's greatest empire; I make new discoveries on each return visit. What you are getting into is a repository with the following departments, each and every one globally outstanding: Coins and Medals, Egyptian Antiquities, Greek and Roman Antiquities, Manuscripts, Medieval Antiquities, Oriental Antiquities, Oriental Printed Books and Manuscripts, Printed Books (including globes and maps), Prints and Drawings, and Western Asiatic Antiquities.

For me, the single most spectacular exhibit is the sculpture from the Parthenon in Athens—the so-called Elgin Marbles—that occupy the entire Duveen Gallery and are arranged in frieze form. They were brought to England in the early nineteenth century by the then-Earl of Elgin, and once one inspects them (they take time, but it is worthwhile), one understands why the Greeks have never forgiven the English for removing them. I am partial, too, to the King's Library, a sumptuous early nineteenth-century chamber created to house books of bibliophile George III and containing such treasures as the Gutenberg Bible, a Shakespeare first folio, and first editions of English classics you remember from school and college. There's so much more: the text of the Magna Carta, exquisite Japanese scrolls and pottery, the Rosetta Stone, Michelangelo drawings, Indian sculpture, mosaics that go back to the Roman occupation of Britain, massive Assyrian sculptures of human-headed animals. If you can, take a peek at the British Library's architectural stunner of a circular Reading Room; its dome—supported by 20 cast-iron girders—was completed in 1857. There are temporary exhibitions, often of Old Master prints from the museum's rich collection.

The *Museum of Mankind*, in its own home at 6 Burlington Gardens, slightly west of Piccadilly Circus, is the Ethnography Department of the British Museum. This museum is visit-worthy if only because it has the finest specimens extant of the art of the old Nigerian kingdom of Benin—not only of wood, but also of iron, bronze, and ivory. There are other exemplary African exhibits. Other galleries turn up such delights as Indonesian puppets, Eskimo carvings, Mexican turquoise mosaics, Australian aboriginal bark painting—the lot masterfully displayed.

Hampton Court Palace (Middlesex) is one of the two out-of-London excursions I include among these dozen requisites. The other is Windsor Castle, and it is touch and go as to which is the more historically important. A strong case could be made for Windsor, but I prefer Hampton Court (partially damaged in a tragic 1986 fire) architecturally. Begun in the early sixteenth century by Cardinal Wolsey, it became a royal residence when the crafty cardinal—in a vain attempt to remain in Henry VIII's good graces—made a gift of it to his king, whose successors lived in it through the reign of the second George, in the mid-eighteenth century.

The medieval portions, built by Wolsey and Henry VIII, form the bulk of this complex of quadrangles. But there are newer and equally splendid late seventeenth-century additions, which William and Mary had Sir Christopher

Wren design. The public has been welcome since Queen Victoria opened the state rooms, but there are a thousand more chambers that make up into a mass of apartments. They are put to good use as "grace and favor" apartments—residences given by the sovereign to the offspring or widows of favored Crown servants.

Memorable interiors are the King's Staircase, with murals by an Italian artist imported by Charles II; the Great Hall, with a Gothic wood ceiling; the also-Gothic Great Watching Chamber; various monarchs' bedrooms, presence chambers, closets, and chapels; the Wren-created Cartoon Gallery, intended for a set of Raphael works but now decorated with tapestries that are copies of the original Raphaels; immense kitchens (it is easy to see how Henry VIII developed his gargantuan appetite); exterior courtyards, both Tudor and Wren; and gardens, most particularly the Maze, which dates to Queen Anne's time.

Windsor Castle (Windsor) is at once the oldest and largest continually inhabited of the royal residences. It has, despite alterations, retained its essentially Norman facade.

Henry II's Round Tower is little changed from the time when it went up in the twelfth century, not long after William the Conqueror founded Windsor as the final link in a chain of fortresses ringing London; Norman walls remain, too. If the castle's interiors are not as consistent in style as its facade, they are hardly without interest. One may inspect the State Apartments daily throughout the year, except when the Royal Family is occupying them, which is usually during April, parts of March, May, June, and December; check before you go.

My favorite rooms are the Queen's Presence Chamber, with its Renaissance painted ceiling, Gobelins tapestries, and Grinling Gibbons carvings; the Queen's Audience Chamber, from the time of Charles II; the eighteenth-century Grand Reception Room—very French and very grand, indeed; the King's State Bedchamber, whose bed was slept in by France's Napoleon III and Eugénie, as guests of Queen Victoria; and St. George's Hall, a Gothic rectangle hung with portraits of sovereigns who have been members of the Windsor-headquartered Order of the Garter. Exemplary also is St. George's Chapel, Perpendicular Gothic. Hardly to be missed are art treasures from the Royal collections at Windsor. Be on the lookout, as you move about, for paintings by a veritable galaxy of masters, including—my arrangement is alphabetical—Canaletto, Clouet, Dürer, Gainsborough, Hogarth, Holbein, Kneller, Lawrence, Lely, Memling, Rembrandt, Rubens, Steen, Van Dyck, and Winterhalter; not to mention drawings—near the entrance—by Leonardo, Carracci, Reni, and Michelangelo, among others. The two-century-old *Castle Hotel* (High Street, Windsor) has a pair of dining rooms and makes for an agreeable lunch pause, as does the *William the Fourth* pub (Thames Street).

The Castle's neighbor is *Eton College*, the kingdom's preeminent boys' school, where not-to-be-missed attractions are the chapel, a Perpendicular Gothic masterwork; the five-century-old Lower School; the somewhat newer Upper School (an upstart dated 1690); a library full of treasures, including a copy of the first printed Bible and some early Shakespeare folios; venerable College Hall and its equally old octagonal kitchen; the multiperiod Cloisters; and the Museum of Eton Life, with exhibits that portray the background of a school that has produced 21 of Britain's prime ministers. The *House on the Bridge* restaurant (Eton High Street), counseled for lunch, affords views of Windsor Castle.

St. Paul's Cathedral (St. Paul's Churchyard): This reputed Wren masterwork is Protestant Britain's answer to Catholic Rome's St. Peter's Basilica. (Wren had visited Rome on his Grand Tour.) St. Paul's is smaller, of course, but this is not to say it even approaches the intimacy of Wren's warm and charming City parish churches, any given half-dozen of which I much prefer. Still, one cannot dismiss St. Paul's—cruciform in shape, with its long nave and monumental dome. There is no gainsaying it is a major monument, nor that it means a great deal to the British people. Its restoration after World War II bombings was an event of the first rank, and so was the 1981 state wedding in St. Paul's, of the Prince of Wales and the former Lady Diana Spencer.

Wren's St. Paul's replaced the earlier "Old" St. Paul's, an absolutely enormous Gothic structure that went up in the eleventh century, was surpassed in size only by the cathedrals of Seville and Milan, and was, from all accounts, magnificent. The Civil War and a fire in 1561 took their toll, and in 1660 Charles II set up a Royal Commission to deal with St. Paul's. Wren came up with a controversial plan to save what remained. But in 1666, the cathedral was totally razed by the Great Fire of London, and Wren produced several brand new designs, one of which was utilized.

By 1697, services were being held in the choir of the new structure. But if St. Paul's was Wren's masterwork, it was also his greatest trial. A faction of MPs determined that work was not progressing rapidly enough and voted to withhold half of Wren's salary until the cathedral was complete. Not until 1711 was he able to petition Queen Anne, then on the throne, that he be paid the arrears due him. Wren himself lived to see St. Paul's nearly finished. In 1714, at the age of eighty-six, he was fired as Surveyor General of the kingdom, but he had by then settled into residence in Hampton Court and made occasional visits into London to inspect his cathedral. He died at the ripe old age of ninety-one and was buried, appropriately enough, in St. Paul's. A tablet above his grave directs the reader, in Latin: "If you seek his monument, look around."

Kensington Palace (Palace Avenue) is still another London landmark with Wren associations—and with William and Mary connections, as well. King William III had Wren make additions and alterations to the place when he took it over in 1689. His successor and sister-in-law, Queen Anne, made enlargements during her reign, as did Anne's successor, George I, who commissioned William Kent to decorate the interiors with sumptuous painted walls and ceilings. The palace is at its most spectacular in the King's Grand Staircase (the work of Wren and Kent), the King's Gallery (with paintings by Rubens and Van Dyck, a fabulous Kent ceiling, and a marble fireplace topped by a Baroque wind-dial), and Kent's opulently embellished Cupola Room.

The parklike gardens are lovely (they include the Orangery that Queen Anne had built), and there are more recent Crown associations, like Queen Victoria's bedroom and nursery; Victoria was born at Kensington, as was Queen Mary, wife of George V, and grandmother of Queen Elizabeth II. (Kensington seems to have spawned strong-willed royal ladies.) Kensington is the only inhabited royal palace in town whose state apartments are visitable, and whenever I have been there it has been a puzzlement as to how few visitors are attracted to a place so rich in historic associations, not to mention historic decorations and furnishings, and the relatively recently installed *Gallery of Court Dress*, with mannequins costumed as courtiers in the course of reigns spanning several centuries. And a surprising number of royals still are in residence.

Banqueting House (Whitehall) is on this honor list of destinations for three reasons. First, it is so convenient that you can easily pop in, in conjunction with a visit to the Changing of the Guards at the Horse Guards. Second, it is a place of visual splendor, for its designer was Inigo Jones, and the immense ceiling is the work of Rubens. And third, because it was a part of a royal palace, in the heart of London, it is absolutely riddled with royal associations. The Banqueting House was completed in 1622, in time to serve as the spot from which Charles I walked to nearby gallows and decapitation. Later, Cromwell moved in, as Lord Protector, remaining until his death in 1658. It was to Whitehall that Charles II returned after he was restored to the throne, and it was here, too, that the Dutchman, Prince William of Orange, and his English wife, Mary, accepted the Crown in 1689. The palace, Banqueting House excepted, burned in 1698, by which time asthmatic William and his Queen had long since moved to Kensington, with its presumed fresher air.

Changing of the Guard: The British sovereign traditionally has two principal guards that parade to musical accompaniment at two locales. The Queen's Guard embraces personnel of the various regiments of a composite body known as the Guards Division, all of whom wear vivid red tunics and towering bearskin caps, but who are members of the Scots, Irish, Welsh, Coldstream, or Grenadier Guards, each with its own uniform variations. They are quartered at Chelsea Barracks and stand duty at Buckingham and St. James's palaces and Clarence House (residence of the Queen Mother). Additionally, until 1973—nocturnally, at least—they guarded the Bank of England (thus the expression "Safe as the Bank of England"). The changing of the Queen's Guard takes place at *Buckingham Palace* at 11:30 A.M. daily in summer and on alternate days the rest of the year.

The other guard of the sovereign is the Queen's Life Guard, whose personnel come from among the two regiments of the Household Cavalry—the Blues and Royals, who wear blue tunics and whose helmets have red plumes; and the Life Guards, with red tunics and white plumes. Their functions include serving as bodyguards to the

sovereign on spectacular al fresco occasions and guard-
ing—while mounted on horseback—*the Horse Guards,
Whitehall,* where the changing ceremony takes place at
11:00 A.M. (10:00 A.M. on Sundays). The Household Cavalry
live at Hyde Park Barracks in Knightsbridge and can be
seen each morning marching through the park to the
Horse Guards. Still other guard-changing spectacles take
place on those days when the guard changes at
Buckingham Palace, at the *Tower of London* (11:30 A.M.) and
at *St. James's Palace* (11:10 A.M.).

National Gallery (Trafalgar Square) is the neoclassic
building that dominates Trafalgar Square. It is so conveniently located that I marvel more of my countrymen don't
go in. It houses one of the superlative collections of Old
Masters, Italians especially, but it is strong, as well, on the
French Impressionists and the English portraitists. The
range, in other words, is European painting from the thirteenth century through the nineteenth, both British and
Continental. There are more than a score of galleries on
the main floor, with a café in the basement. The Italian
medieval work—Masolino's *Saints John the Baptist and
Jerome,* for example—is a joy. One sees, as well, Bronzino
and Titian, Bellini and Botticelli, among the Italians, who
are possibly no better represented anywhere else outside
Italy; Vermeer and Rembrandt (represented by a whopping 19 paintings), among the Dutch; Goya, Murillo, and
Velázquez, among the Spaniards. The Golden English
eighteenth century of Reynolds, Gainsborough, Hogarth,
and their contemporaries is strongly represented, along
with later British greats like Constable and Turner. The
eighteenth-century French—Watteau and Chardin—are
present, and there are many galleries of later French
work—Degas, Manet, Cézanne, Seurat, Monet, Renoir.
Once hooked on this brilliant collection, I wager you'll find
yourself returning to it on every London visit; I do.

Cabinet War Rooms (Clive Steps, beneath a statue of Lord Clive, at the end of King Charles Street) are as good a reason as any to stroll alongside the splendidly detailed Victorian ministries of Whitehall—a part of town too often neglected by visitors. This subterranean complex— relatively recently restored by, and under the aegis of, the also-too-neglected Imperial War Museum (below)— comprises a suite of 19 chambers wherein His Majesty's Government, under Prime Minister Winston Churchill, conducted the Second World War between late August in 1939 and the Japanese surrender in 1945, functioning even during Nazi air raids. You see the Cabinet Room in which a hundred meetings took place during the height of the Blitz. The Transatlantic Telephone Room is the place from which Churchill spoke to President Roosevelt in the White House. The Map Room was the war planners' nerve center. Throughout, designers have placed authentic equipment of the era—bulky, old-fashioned British telephones, chairs and desks, file cabinets and memo pads, teacups and lamps, and even cigarette packs, matchboxes, and newspapers. Churchill's bedroom is perhaps the most memorable of the interiors; on view is the PM's chamber pot (there was no modern sanitation), along with a legend explaining that he so disliked using the pot that he slept above-ground whenever possible. World War II constituted Britain's finest hour of the modern era; a self-guided tour of these remarkable rooms helps explain why. (Unless hours change, the rooms are open to visitors on Sunday mornings—when just about nothing else in London is, churches excepted.)

ARCHITECTURAL LONDON: AN ALPHABETICAL SAMPLER

Of the great cities, none is quite the delightful architectural mix of many eras in quite the same way as London. Gothic, Renaissance, Georgian, Regency, Victorian, Edwardian, and, yes, our own era, as well; London has them all.

Not everything in my alphabetical selection below is open to the public; some places are only partially open, and some are no more than monuments of interest to passersby.

Bank of England (Threadneedle Street) gives its name—simply The Bank—to the busy City area it dominates structurally and as the unique bank that serves both the British government and the private banking industry. The bank itself, though mostly modern and mostly unvisitable to the public, retains the one-story, wall-like facade that Sir John Soane (whose house, not far distant, is recommended on another page) designed for it in the early nineteenth century in neoclassic style. Behind is a modern structure. Only the entrance hall is open to visitors.

Bridging the Thames are mostly modern structures. The most famous, the one that was falling down in our childhood nursery rhyme—*London Bridge*—did just that. Or at least its early nineteenth-century successor did. Too venerable to cope with modern traffic, it suffered the indignity of being taken apart and transported piece by piece to Arizona, where it has been reerected, to be succeeded by a more functional replacement. *Tower Bridge* is a charming neo-Gothic structure dating only to the turn of the century, with the Tower of London as a backdrop, and a glass-enclosed pedestrian walkway that opened in 1982, which is reached by elevator from the bridge's North Tower—but only after you've paid a substantial admission fee. *Westminster Bridge*, nineteenth century and nondescript, is highly efficient. So, for that matter, is the much newer (pre-World War II, albeit romantically named) *Waterloo Bridge*. The view is nice when you find yourself crossing it,

en route to or from Royal Festival Hall. And the vista is
equally impressive for pedestrians traversing *Southwark
Bridge*, as nice a way as any to approach Southwark Cathedral, on the South Bank.

Buckingham Palace (The Mall) is, of course, the sovereign's London home and a household word throughout the world. It is named for the Duke of Buckingham and
Chandos, who erected it in the eighteenth century, selling
it to George III in 1761. George IV had his architect, John
Nash, remodel it in the early nineteenth century. Queen
Victoria—who eventually took it over as her town
house—made changes, as did her grandson, George V, as
recently as 1913.

The only parts of the palace open to the public are the
Queen's Gallery and the Royal Mews (see Museumgoer's
London in this chapter). The setting—Buckingham Palace
Gardens, an extension of Green and St. James's parks—is
exceptionally capacious and little short of inspired, considering that the palace is in the heart of a great urban
center.

Should you be invited inside, rooms to see are the
throne-dominated red and gold State Ballroom, where
state banquets are held and where the Queen conducts in-
vestitures and other ceremonies; the Throne Room, with
its frieze of the Wars of the Roses; the Nash-designed
Music Room, with a circular dome supported by Corinthian columns; and the White Drawing Room—with gilded
plasterwork, yellow draperies, and French and Regency
furnishings. And there is a chance of a Palace invitation;
the guest list for each of the royal garden parties totals
9,000.

Chelsea Royal Hospital (Royal Hospital and Ormonde
West roads) is one of the anachronisms that make London
so interesting. Charles II founded it as a veterans' hospital

in the seventeenth century—much like the Louis XIV-established Les Invalides in Paris. It is still another Wren work with additions by Robert Adam, among others. Every year, on "the nearest convenient Sunday to the birthday [May 29] of his Gracious Majesty King Charles II, Our Royal Founder" (as the printed program puts it), the hospital observes Founder's Day in its splendid chapel. Preceding the services, the Governor of the Hospital, in plumed hat, reviews red-coated inmates at a parade on the grounds. At the Chapel service, there is a fanfare by military trumpeters, and prayers include one taken from the 1662 edition of the *Book of Common Prayer*, which gives thanks "for the Restoration of the Royal Family." Not every Sunday service at the hospital is so elaborate, but the hospital is never without interest. Great Hall and Chapel are open to visitors, and so is the Council Chamber, with portraits by Lely, Kneller, and Van Dyck.

Clubs, mostly for gents, but usually with privileges for their ladies, are a tradition that, for better or worse, the British have exported to distant corners of the planet, not excluding nonwhite ex-colonies where dark-skinned locals were rarely, if ever, admitted, except as servants. Surely a case could be made for the role of the club in the dissolution of the Empire; I shall not forget an unavoidable stay at the whites-only English Club, in preindependence Zanzibar. But suffice it, at this point, to make mention of the locale of a few of the clubs and to admire them for their architecture, if not necessarily for their exclusivity. St. James's Street, leading from Piccadilly down to St. James's Palace, is the site of a choice trio—the late-eighteenth-century *Brooks* and its also-venerable across-the-street neighbors, *Boodles* and *Whites*. Pall Mall—the name is believed to have come from a Restoration game, *paille-maille*—which runs perpendicular to St. James's Street, is almost exclusively clubs: the *Reform* and the *Travellers',* both by the same Sir Charles Barry who designed the great staircase hall of neighboring Lancaster House; the *Oxford and Cambridge*, with its largely academic membership (and super roast beef and Yorkshire pudding in its restaurant, if you're invited), and a number of others, from the *Conservative* at St. James's Street to the *Athenaeum* at Pall Mall's other extremity, Waterloo Place.

Downing Street, a narrow thoroughfare that lies between St. James's Park and Whitehall, with government ministries all about, is most celebrated for the house at No. 10, which has been the home of prime ministers since George II offered it to Sir Robert Walpole well over two centuries ago. Within is the street-floor Cabinet Room. Since Walpole's time, there have been a number of renovations, including one by the noted Sir John Soane in 1825. No. 10 is not the only noteworthy house on the street. No. 11 is where Chancellors of the Exchequeur live, and No. 12 is the official digs of the Chief Government Whip, a not unimportant parliamentary political leader. None of this trio of houses is open to the public, but a stroll past can yield glimpses of government brass and their colleagues, or at the very least members of the press *waiting* for government brass and their colleagues.

Lambeth Palace (Lambeth Road) is an absolutely super Middle Ages cluster. It's the London seat of the Archbishops of Canterbury (the top administrators of the Church of England) and has been these many centuries. There's a formidable gatehouse, an imposing Great Hall, and a venerable detached chapel. The problem is open hours; be sure to double-check before you go.

Law Courts (Strand) comprise a splendidly sprawling Victorian Gothic cluster (Her Majesty dedicated them in 1882) and are officially the Royal Courts of Justice. Cases tried are civil and are usually open to visitors; Monday through Friday 10:30 A.M.–1:00 P.M. and 2:00 P.M.–6:00 P.M. Pop in to have a look.

Lincoln's Inn and the other Inns of Court: Lincoln's Inn (Chancery Lane) is a sanctuary of tranquility in the midst of the City: half an hour's stroll through it is indeed a London treat. It is one of the so-called Inns of Court, which traditionally control the practice of law in England and which include resident quarters for member-lawyers, as well as other facilities. Lincoln's Inn (named for a medieval Earl of Lincoln) goes back to the fifteenth century. What you want to see are Old Hall, built the year Columbus discovered our shores; New Hall, late nineteenth century; the library, opened by Queen Victoria in 1845; and the much older Chapel, which was consecrated in 1623, with poet-cleric John Donne at the opening service. Few monarchs have not participated in a Lincoln's Inn activity of one sort or other. And no less than nine prime ministers have been Lincoln's Inn-ers, Walpole through Asquith.

The other Inns of Court are City neighbors of Lincoln's Inn. *Gray's Inn* (Holborn) is an also-medieval complex. The Great Hall, dating to Tudor times, is exemplary, and so are the library, chapel, and gardens. The *Inner and Middle Temples* (Middle Temple Lane) share the same complex, as well as the *Temple Church* (see London Churches: After the Abbey and St. Paul's, in this chapter). The Great Hall of each Temple is its masterwork.

London County Hall (Belvedere Road) is a nine-story, 1,500-room, nineteen-twenties neo-Renaissance pile, distinguished by a curved colonnaded front. Situation is Thames-front. Worth seeing are the octagonal Council Chamber (the council's meetings are usually held on alternate Tuesday afternoons) and the library.

Mansion House (Mansion House Street) is the Georgian building that for long has served as the official home of the City of London's Lord Mayor. Its most distinctive feature is a Corinthian portico, from which incumbents watch parades and make speeches. Major public room is the misnamed Egyptian Hall (its design is neoclassic). There is, as well, the minuscule Lord Mayor's Court of Justice, still in session daily, with His Worship or an alderman presiding and with cells directly below-stairs.

Marble Arch is a detached segment of Buckingham Palace that George IV's architect, John Nash, intended originally as the principal gateway. It was not broad enough for royal coaches, so it was moved to a less strategic point some years later. Finally, in 1851, it was transplanted to the site where Park Lane and Oxford Street intersect, where it has remained ever since.

The Monument (Fish Street Hill)—and that is its proper name—is a freestanding column, extending from a point on the Thames's north bank, in the City, some 202 feet heavenwards. It is believed to have been originally designed by scientist Robert Hooke, but Sir Christopher Wren was involved in its construction. It went up in 1671, and its function is to commemorate the horrendous Great Fire of 1666, which destroyed much of the city, including many medieval churches, some half a hundred of which were replaced by Wren structures. If you have the strength or the youth or both, you may ascend to the summit; there are 311 steps.

Old Bailey (On the street named for it) is not, alas, very old. The building itself, that is. It is mostly turn-of-century, with a dome apparently intended to complement that of neighboring St. Paul's. The business at hand is the trial of criminal cases in this most celebrated of the world's criminal courts. Visitors are welcome, usually mornings and afternoons, Monday through Friday. Every so often, officers of the court toss dried flowers on the floor—a symbolic carryover from the time when the court was connected with the infamous (and smelly) Newgate Prison, which stood on its site.

Royal Exchange (Cornhill) is no longer an exchange but rather the home of an insurance company. It's the third such structure on the site and is mid-nineteenth century, with a Corinthian portico (from which new sovereigns were traditionally proclaimed) and inner quadrangle that used to be where exchange business was transacted, but is now the site of exhibitions. The exchange is nicely combined with nearby *Guildhall* (Cheapside), the City's City Hall, going back six centuries, with an impressive Great Hall (the site of major City ceremonies) and an art gallery.

St. James's Palace complex: Sovereigns have not lived in St. James's Palace for over a century, but tradition dies hard in Britain, and foreign ambassadors to the Crown are still accredited to the Court of St. James. The front facade, looking out onto St. James's Street and the men's clubs that line it, is the old Tudor-era gatehouse of the palace and the oldest part of it remaining. The part of the palace called York House is the residence of the Duke of Kent. Another section includes "grace and favor" apartments, awarded by the Crown to the families of loyal servants, and the Chapel Royal (see London Churches: After the Abbey and St. Paul's, in this chapter). The palace is not open to the public, but its courtyard is and makes for a rewarding stroll. The setting is, after all, the onetime home of Henry VIII and his children, Edward VI, Bloody Mary, and Elizabeth I, not to mention other sovereigns through to the last century's William IV and Queen Adelaide. Ever since, oaths of office have been administered to monarchs at St. James's, including Elizabeth II in 1952, and it is from the palace balcony that, on the death of the sovereign, the traditional proclamation is made: "The King is dead! Long live the King!"

Marlborough House is named for the first Duke of Marlborough, although it was the pet project of his Duchess, Sarah, who commissioned Sir Christopher Wren to design it as the couple's town house, while Sir John Vanbrugh, with whom the tempestuous Sarah had fallen out, was putting up the Blenheim Palace she came to despise. Marlboroughs stayed on until George IV's time, when the Royal Family took title. After William IV died, his widow, Dowager Queen Adelaide, moved in upon the accession of her niece, Victoria, to the throne.

Later, Marlborough House was home to Victoria's eldest son, while he was Prince of Wales. When the Prince of Wales became Edward VII and moved to Buckingham Palace, his younger son, the Duke of York later, George V—replaced him. When George acceded, his widowed mother, Queen Alexandra, succeeded him at Marlborough House; and upon the death of George V in 1936, George's widow, Queen Mary, returned to the house she had known as the Duchess of York, remaining there—the place furnished with the fine antiques she had collected, but still with no modern plumbing—until she died in 1953. A few years later, Mary's granddaughter, Elizabeth II, signed a Royal Warrant turning the house over to the British Government, so that it could be converted for the use of Commonwealth prime ministers.

Consequently—and rather sadly—the house bears little resemblance to its Wren period or even to more recent royal occupancies. Still, plasterwork, fireplaces, and ceilings of principal main-floor rooms are intact, and so are paintings depicting the Duke of Marlborough's battles, in the main hall (Battle of Blenheim), main staircase (Battle of

Ramillies), and east staircase (Battle of Malplaquet). Upstairs, all the rooms, save an Edwardian smoking room,
have been turned into workaday offices. Queen Mary's
sitting room—the historic one in which her son, Edward
VIII, revealed to his mother and sister his plans to
abdicate—is now a steel-and-leatherette conference
room.

Lancaster House went up in 1825 for the then-Duke of
York. In 1827, it became the property of the Marquess of
Stafford, who added a Staircase Hall as high as the house
itself and illuminated from above by an absolutely enormous lantern. Corinthian columns support the elaborate
ceiling from the second-floor level, and the walls are surfaced ingeniously in *faux-marbre* inset with a series of Italian copies of Veronese paintings. Lancaster House, since
1912, has been the property of the British Government,
which uses it for luncheons and receptions. The fanciest
post-World War II event was Prime Minister Sir Winston
Churchill's luncheon in the Great Gallery honoring
Queen Elizabeth II on her Coronation.

Clarence House, just beyond St. James's, is the same age
as Lancaster House and is named for its first resident, King
William IV, who was Duke of Clarence at the time; it has
been a royal residence ever since. Current occupant is
Queen Elizabeth, the Queen Mother, who replaced her
daughter Queen Elizabeth II and her son-in-law, the Duke
of Edinburgh, as residents when they succeeded her at
Buckingham Palace after the death of King George VI. Not
open to the public.

Scotland Yard (Broadway): The "New," which became part
of Scotland Yard's title when it moved in 1890 from
Whitehall, has never been more apt. Scotland Yard, or
more accurately the Metropolitan Police, moved from its
atmospheric Victorian building on the Victoria Embankment, to its *really* new quarters—in 1967. To a passerby,

the Yard looks like an ordinary glass and concrete office tower. But I am told that within are the very latest in laboratories, TV and radio communications, and the noted Criminal Records Office.

Stock Exchange (Old Broad Street) is, along with the neighboring Bank of England, the financial core of the Commonwealth. Securities-market buffs will enjoy the view from the balcony of the trading sessions on the floor, Mondays through Fridays, traditionally from 10:00 A.M. to 3:15 P.M.

University of London (Bloomsbury): Overshadowed by Oxford and Cambridge, both of which are centuries older, the relatively modern (1836) University of London is bound to be underappreciated. It has some 36,000 students in 35 buildings and 14 specialized institutes, and its principal buildings are in Bloomsbury, near the British Museum. Built with a Rockefeller Foundation grant in the nineteen-twenties, they were dedicated by George V in 1933 and include the 210-foot-high Tower, a library of 900,000 volumes, and the Senate House, for administration. There are two first-rank museums, later recommended: Courtauld Institute and Percival David Foundation of Chinese Art. University College, older than the University of London, of which it is now a part, goes back to 1828 and has its own home on Gower Street. It has some 5,000 students in a number of faculties, including the Slade School of Art. Also on Gower Street are the globally renowned London School of Tropical Medicine and Royal Academy of Dramatic Art.

LONDON CHURCHES: AFTER THE ABBEY AND ST. PAUL'S

Next to Rome, London is Europe's greatest church city,

surpassing Paris and, indeed, all of the other European capitals. Norman (the British way of saying Romanesque), Gothic, Renaissance, Baroque, even a cathedral in Byzantine style: London has them all.

A DOZEN-PLUS ALL-LONDON STANDOUTS

Southwark Cathedral (London Bridge) does not attempt to compete with Westminster Abbey, although perhaps it should. Across the river, in South London, it was antedated by an earlier Norman church, but its more or less present Gothic look dates from the twelfth through fifteenth centuries, when the elaborate choir and the fine transept were constructed. The high nave is actually Victorian. Although Southwark has been a cathedral or, in other words, the seat of a bishop in charge of a diocese, only since the turn of the present century, it is not without a rich history. During the unhappy reign of Henry VIII's elder daughter, the Catholic Bloody Mary, Protestant martyrs were tried in Southwark. James VI was married there, and John Harvard, founder of the American university bearing his name, was baptized there (the Harvard Chapel of the Cathedral honors him).

Westminster Cathedral (Ashley Place): There are some six million Roman Catholics in Britain, and enough of them live in and around London for it to constitute an archdiocese headed by an archbishop of cardinal's rank, whose seat is turn-of-the-century Westminster Cathedral. This Byzantine beauty is London's least-known major church, and more's the pity. Although the cathedral opened in 1903, it still is not completed. Only half of the dozen chapels that ring the nave are decorated with the mosaics intended for them. Length is 360 feet. The nave is 117 feet high, and the campanile (to which, please note, there is an elevator to take visitors to an observation tower that affords a smashing view of London) is 273 feet high. Capacity is 2,000, all seated and able to see the sumptuous high altar, over which, suspended from the ceiling, is an immense red and gold cross.

St. Bartholomew the Great (West Smithfield) is essentially Romanesque and, except for St. John the Evangelist Chapel in the Tower of London, the oldest in town. It is a neighbor of both St. Bartholomew's Hospital (the oldest in London) and the smaller St. Bartholomew the Less Church. St. Bartholomew the Great goes back to the early twelfth century, and, although much of it was destroyed at the time of the Reformation, enough remains—the masterful choir, part of the nave, and other architectural treasures—to make the church one of the first rank. An all-Britain standout.

St. Margaret's Westminster (Parliament Square) is, because it is part of the Westminster Abbey complex, overshadowed by the Abbey. But it has been the official church of the House of Commons for four of its ten centuries, and, perhaps even more significant to readers of society pages, it is the venue for fashionable weddings; St. Margaret's bridegrooms have included Samuel Pepys, John Milton, and Sir Winston Churchill.

Brompton Oratory (Brompton Road) is, like Westminster Cathedral, Catholic and is, again like Westminster Cathedral, of a refreshingly uncommon-to-London style. You have the not unpleasant feeling, on an oratory visit, that you're in Rome or Florence. It is a late nineteenth-century variation of Italian Renaissance, and it is noted for its music.

Chapel Royal of St. James's Palace (Pall Mall) is the only part of the palace open to the public and then only for Sunday services. Its chef d'oeuvre is the ceiling, which Holbein is believed to have painted and which shows easily discernible royal initials—"H" for Henry VIII and "A" believed to stand for Anne of Cleves, Wife No. 4, to whom Henry was married in 1540, the date appearing on the ceiling. Other queens were married in the chapel, too, not least among them being Victoria, three centuries to the year after Anne and Henry.

Queen's Chapel, Marlborough House (Pall Mall) is a lovely Inigo Jones work named for Queen Henrietta Maria, wife of Charles I, who inaugurated it. Choir boys' gowns are as they have been for centuries, and the royal pews are original.

Chapel Royal of St. Peter ad Vincula, in the Tower of London (Tower Hill), is the oldest of England's chapels royal, dating to the twelfth century, and where many sovereigns worshiped, including two—Queen Anne Boleyn and Queen Catherine Howard—just before they were executed. The Gothic look of the place remains. The choir's musical skills are esteemed; visitors are welcome at Sunday services and do not have to pay the usual Tower admission fee.

Chelsea Royal Hospital Chapel (Royal Hospital Road), like the hospital itself, was designed by Wren, with its chief decorative element a massive mural called *The Last Muster.* A Sunday service—with the pensioners in their traditional uniform and the choir in equally old style vestments—is a treat.

Guards' Chapel, Wellington Barracks (Birdcage Walk), is essentially post-World War II, for the beautiful original was badly bombed. Some of the old remains, though, and there is always music by one of the various Guards' regiment bands at Sunday services, to which visitors are welcome.

Temple Church (Temple) is the place of worship shared by the Inner Temple and the Middle Temple, two of the four London Inns of Court. It goes back some eight hundred years, combining Gothic and Romanesque features impressively, with a chancel of the former period appended to the original round church of the latter.

All Souls' (Langham Place at Regent Street) was designed by John Nash, the Regency architect. It was war-damaged but the restoration is commendable, and the interior is quite as handsome as the near-circular exterior is distinctive.

St. Peter's (Eaton Square) is one to have a look at when you are inspecting Belgravia. A landmark of rectangular Eaton Square, it is a late nineteenth-century neoclassic structure, understandably popular for *haute monde* weddings.

St. Mary Abbots (Kensington High Street) is an oasis of quiet and beauty in the heart of Kensington. It is Victorian Gothic, with an unusually tall spire (278 feet) and, among other attributes, an unusual cloistered walkway. Pop in for a rest, while doing the Kensington shops.

TEN BY WREN

Aside from the earlier-recommended St. Paul's, Sir Christopher Wren designed more than 50 seventeenth-century London churches, most in the City. By no means have all survived World War II intact; of some, only towers or less remain. Others have been beautifully restored. What follows are ten Wren churches that I especially like; *do take in any others that you pass by.* They all feature weekday lunchtime services and concerts, and every single one is a jewel. Only the first is not in the City.

St. James's (Piccadilly): Devastation during World War II was almost complete. The restoration, with the exception of an unfortunate Victorian stained-glass window behind the altar, has been first-rate, with the glorious arched ceiling as it was and the baroque organ rebuilt (Grinling Gibbons carved the gilt cherubs atop it). There's a worth-knowing-about café, convenient for casual lunches.

St. Bride's (Fleet Street) is a restoration of a Wren church that was the eighth on the site and below which have been found the remains of a Roman house. St. Bride's worshipers have included Chaucer, Shakespeare, Milton, Evelyn, and Pepys. The restoration was made possible by contributions from Fleet Street newspaper neighbors. But the American press has a soft spot for St. Bride's, too. Among the memorial plaques is one given to honor U.S. journalists who lost their lives in the course of their work abroad, by the Overseas Press Club of America, through the efforts of a colleague and friend of mine, the late Madeline Dane Ross.

St. Clement Danes (Strand) is, like later-described St. Mary-le-Strand, on an island in the Strand. It is less harrowing to reach, however. Post-World War II restoration was brilliant, and in the process the Royal Air Force adopted the church as its official place of worship. This is the church of "Oranges and Lemons say the bells of St. Clement's," and the nursery rhyme is commemorated annually at a youngsters' service. Withal, the interior is what makes it most stand out—pulpit, painted reredos, U.S. Air Force-donated organ, and ceiling supported by Corinthian columns.

St. James, Garlickhythe (Upper Thames Street) seems dwarfed by its substantial steeple and is a surprise within, for its ceiling is the highest of any in the City. Decor is elegantly simple. Hythe, I learned from the verger, used to mean cove—a place where ships tied up and, in this instance, one assumes, where their chief cargo was garlic.

St. Lawrence, Jewry (Gresham Street), so named because of its situation in an ancient ghetto quarter, is extra-substantial Wren, in keeping with its designation as the official church of the Corporation, or Council, of the City of London. Its lengthy rectangular interior is accented by a series of handsome brass chandeliers, splendid plaster-work, and typical dark-wood pews, altar, and organ. The City's landmark, Guildhall, is next door. A dazzler.

St. Mary Abchurch (Abchurch Lane, off Cannon Street) is distinguished by a painted dome that dominates the squarish interior, contrast coming from white walls and the dark wood of the superb Grinling Gibbons-carved altar.

St. Benet, Paul's Wharf (Upper Thames Street), has a graceful exterior, with garlands of stone atop each clear-paned window. Within, the feeling is one of great height. Ceiling plasterwork is exceptional. If you don't understand the language being spoken, fear not. Services are conducted in Welsh.

St. Mary-le-Bow (Cheapside) is oddly Italianate Wren—light walls and ceilings are of a piece. A great gold crucifix hangs from the ceiling. Floors are black and white marble. The feeling is of luxuriant space. And the crypt is Norman.

St. Mary Aldermary (Watling Street) is a Wren shocker, the master in a Gothic mood; and it works, if one overlooks a bit of well-meant Victorian gussying up. Wren's ceiling is his version of Gothic fan vaulting. There are side aisles framed by Gothic arches, and the other Wren-Gothic touches are charming, too.

St. Stephen Walbrook (Walbrook) is another Italianate Wren, with a series of 16 columns lining the inside of the oblong interior and framing an immense coffered dome. Oddly, somewhat heavily handsome—but with style.

A QUARTET BY JAMES GIBBS

James Gibbs's output in the first half of the eighteenth century embraced ten London churches, not to mention important work at both Cambridge and Oxford. He was later than Wren and was obviously influenced by that master, with the result handsomely and typically Georgian. Gibbs's work, in turn, inspired countless designers of the steepled churches that became a commonplace of colonial America.

St. Martin-in-the Fields (Trafalgar Square) was completed by Gibbs in 1726, and George I was its first church warden. His coat of arms remains in the church above the chancel arch. To this day, St. Martin's is the sovereign's parish church. It is, as well, the official church of the Admiralty. (There are both Royal and Admiralty pews.) There is a sumptuous gilded and cream ceiling, supported by rows of Corinthian columns. The pulpit has Grinling Gibbons carving.

Grosvenor Chapel (South Audley Street) is just off Grosvenor Square, site of the American Embassy and for that reason a gathering place for many Americans during World War II; a plaque within records the special American association.

St. Mary-le-Strand (Strand) is, rather ingeniously, built upon an island in one of London's most horrendously traffic-filled thoroughfares, so that by the time you are able to cross the street to gain admittance, you feel constrained to offer thanks in the church for having arrived safely, at the same time praying that you will be able to make an equally safe exit from the little island to the across-the-street sidewalk. Within, a gilded ceiling shelters a neoclassic interior. En route out, before you step into that traffic, look up at the handsome white steeple.

St. Peter's (Vere Street) is another small Gibbs treasure and still substantially Georgian. St. Peter's, completed in 1724, antedated St. Martin-in-the-Fields and is a kind of St. Martin in miniature.

Additional, Mostly Anglican Churches

St. Etheldreda's (Ely Place) is the first pre-Reformation church to be returned from Anglican to Roman Catholic jurisdiction and stands in a little-visited City cul-de-sac. It is a Gothic treasure, well restored after World War II. The west window, originally fourteenth century, is said to be one of the biggest in all London. There are, as well, a little cloister and a crypt.

St. Olave, Hart Street (off Fenchurch Street), is a beautiful Gothic church entered through its own well-enclosed yard (the benches are nice for a rest on a busy sightseeing day). The building is essentially fifteenth century—with stone walls, Gothic arched windows and aisles, and a beamed ceiling. Mr. and Mrs. Samuel Pepys were members of the parish (there is a bust of Mrs. Pepys erected by her husband).

St. Helen's, Bishopsgate (Bishopsgate), is another basically Gothic church. It is more elaborate than St. Olave, with Renaissance accents and additions from other eras, even including a Victorian screen. The flattish timbered roof evokes medieval times; so, for that matter, does the church as a whole, its more modern appurtenances notwithstanding.

St. Dunstan-in-the-West (Fleet Street) is early nineteenth-century neo-Gothic, with a winning octagonal shape, a wedding-cake tower, and an interior more comfortable and inviting than distinguished. Agreeable for a pause after, say, Dr. Johnson's House, in nearby Gough Square.

St. Botolph Without Aldgate (Aldgate High Street): Botolph, the patron saint of English travelers, a kind of U.K. St. Christopher, was English-born (seventh century) and so popular that in the City alone are three churches named for him, two with locations so similar-sounding that they can be confusing. (One is at Bishopsgate, but the other two are at Aldersgate and Aldgate.) All three are of interest, but I have selected Aldgate; it's mostly mid-eighteenth century and high-ceilinged, with Doric columns for support.

OTHER LONDON PLACES OF WORSHIP

Bloomsbury Central Baptist Church, Shaftesbury Avenue; *First Church of Christ Scientist*, Sloane Terrace; *Westminster Congregational Chapel*, Buckingham Gate, Westminster; *West London Synagogue* (Reformed), Upper Berkeley Street; *Central Synagogue* (Orthodox), Great Portland Street; *St.*

Anne and St. Agnes Lutheran Church (seventeenth century), Gresham Street; *John Wesley's Chapel* (Methodist, built in 1778), City Road; *Regent Square Presbyterian Church*, Regent Square; *St. Sophia Cathedral* (Greek Orthodox), Moscow Road; *Westminster Friends Meeting House*, St. Martin's Lane; *Salvation Army Regent Hall*, Oxford Street; *Spiritualist Association*, Belgrave Square; *Hindu Center*, Grafton Terrace; *Central Mosque*, Park Road; *Sikh Temple*, Sinclair Road; *Buddhist Society*, Eccleston Square.

MUSEUMGOER'S LONDON: SOME SELECTED FAVORITES

The British Museum, perhaps more than any other, reflects the acquisitions made available to a major imperial power. It, the National Gallery, and the National Portrait Gallery—the last-mentioned because it sets the stage for London—are among my earlier Baker's Dozen London attractions. But they are only a starter, for museums. I have selected additional museums and memorial houses that I especially like.

Tate Gallery (Millbank) is outstanding for its specialties. British painting from the Renaissance onward and modern work from the Impressionists through to, say, last week. In the superlative English section, there are fine Peter Lelys, Hogarths, Gainsboroughs, and Reynoldses. But the star of the Tate is J. M. W. Turner, the early nineteenth-century English painter who was a good half-century ahead of his time and who is better represented at this museum than at any other. There are exceptionally strong Constable and Blake sections, too; stellar French works—Manet through Matisse; and frequently excellent short-term exhibits. The museum building is attractive and a joy to explore. In a word, one of Europe's most important collections.

Victoria and Albert Museum (Cromwell Road)—the "V and A" to Londoners—is a unit of the group of South Kensington museums devised by Prince Albert, after his Great Exhibition of 1851. Victoria herself laid the corner-stone in 1899, not long before she died; her son, Edward VII, opened the building in 1909—not long before he died. The V and A is a massive and magnificent repository of British *and* Continental decorative and fine arts. Emphasis is on European work from the Middle Ages onward. Not unexpectedly, English furniture and furnishings are par-ticularly strong. But there are treasures ranging from paintings by Raphael to Renaissance ship models of solid gold. Not-to-be-missed exhibits are the room settings—a room from Clifford's Inn, London, of the seventeenth cen-tury; a room from Henrietta Place, London, designed by James Gibbs; a room from a house in Hatton Garden, Lon-don, of the eighteenth century; the music room from Nor-folk House, London, the work of James Wyatt; another chamber by Robert Adam; a Regency room by Thomas Hope; and other settings illustrating the contribution of designers ranging from exuberant William Kent to re-strained William Morris.

Courtauld Institute Galleries (Woburn Square) is one of London's—and all Europe's—best-kept museum surpris-es. A unit of the University of London and with a Blooms-bury location near the British Museum, the Courtauld—one floor up in a nondescript building via an enormous and rather creaky self-service elevator—is an absolute treasure. There are three major collections. Best known is of Impressionists and post-Impressionists—the collection of the late Samuel Courtauld, an industrialist. Manet's *A Bar at the Folies-Bergère* in itself makes a visit worthwhile. But consider also Toulouse-Lautrec's *La Chambre Separée*, Monet's *Vase des Fleurs*, Renoir's *La Loge*, and Gauguin's *Haymaking*. Old Masters include rich Italian representation—Botticelli, Bellini, Veronese, Tintoretto, for example—but other painters' work, too. I particularly like the Cranach *Adam and Eve* and a lady called Mrs. Malcolm painted by Sir Henry Raeburn.

Buckingham Palace museums (Buckingham Palace Road): British sovereigns can be excused for not opening their London home to the public; none in Europe, save the Swedish monarchs, open the town palaces they live in to visitors. Still, if Buckingham proper is not open to the public, two parts of it are. The first and more visited of the two is the *Queen's Gallery*, occupying part of a former chapel and entered from Buckingham Palace Road. Space being relatively small, the exhibition policy is eminently sound. There is no permanent exhibit. Rather, the show changes once or twice a year and consists of groupings of works from Her Majesty's priceless private collections, the range, Old Masters to royal portraits. Not to be missed.

The other palace museum, the *Royal Mews*, is entered by its own impressive gateway, also on Buckingham Palace Road. This is Her Majesty's stables, with which is incorporated a museum of royal coaches. There are other coach museums in Europe—those of Lisbon and Munich's Nymphenburg Palace come to mind. What makes the Mews unique is that the coaches, most of them at least, are still in use when the occasion demands—the Gold State Coach, for example, dates from George III's reign and still is used at coronations. The Irish State Coach goes to work every year when the sovereign opens Parliament. The State Landau is used regularly when Queen Elizabeth fetches visiting foreign heads of state from railway stations. There are a lot more, and there are, as well, the comfortably housed royal horses, the corps of coachmen and grooms who headquarter here, and historic photographs of monarchs or their families atop the backs of their steeds.

Wallace Collection (Manchester Square) occupies Hertford House, eighteenth-century dwelling of the dukes of Manchester. It has an ambience not unlike that of New York's Frick Collection, except that Hertford House gives the impression of having been considerably more lived in. The Wallace Collection was a gift to the British people from the widow of Sir Richard Wallace, who, with his ancestors, had collected it mostly in France. Baroque paintings are the chief lure—the great Dutch and Flemish artists are all present, Rembrandt and Steen, Rubens and Van Dyck. But the French—Boucher, Fragonard, Watteau—are big, especially those of the eighteenth century. And so are Spaniards, like Murillo and Velázquez, and the English, like Gainsborough, Reynolds, and Romney. Painting is only part of the collection; there is armor, for example, and perfectly beautiful eighteenth-century French furniture.

Museum of London (The Barbican) is a repository of Londoniana through the ages. You start with the prehistoric era, continue through the Dark Ages, the formative period of Roman London, or *Londinium,* and continue on through medieval, Tudor, later-Renaissance, Georgian, Regency, Victorian-Edwardian, and contemporary London, the last represented by, among other objects, Queen Elizabeth II's coronation robe. There are ancient coins, precious glass, furniture (including the bed slept in by King James II and his alliteratively named Queen, Mary of Modena), and a Victorian fire engine. Setting is a boldly contemporary pavilion, with access by a series of ramps and walkways from the street.

Sir John Soane's Museum (13 Lincoln's Inn Fields) is where the prolific architect lived the last quarter-century (1813–37) of a long life. The setting is an eighteenth-century City square, and the house was designed by Sir John as both home and museum. Contents include an astonishing variety of art and antiques: Roman relics, Egyptian works, Greek sculpture, Italian art, and other paintings—England's Turner, as well as Venice's Canaletto, not to mention a Lawrence of Sir John himself. Most fascinating are two Hogarth series—*The Election* and *The Rake's Progress*. They are explained in detail by a resident guard, standing before a prominent wall sign directing visitors not to tip their lecturer. There will, *indeed*, always be an England.

Wellington Museum (Apsley House, Hyde Park Corner) was the first Duke of Wellington's London home. Robert Adam was the original designer. Most remarkable single exhibit is in the dining room—a service of silver plate from the Regent of Portugal, which took well over a hundred silversmiths several years to create. The entrance hall catches one up with its larger-than-life statue of Napoleon clad in a fig leaf. There are other similarly eccentric treasures. Then one moves along to the house's oddly uncelebrated treasures: its paintings. Fact of the matter is that Apsley House shelters a major London collection: Italians, including Correggio, Bassano, and Pannini; Spaniards, including Velázquez, Murillo, and a Goya of the first Duke of Wellington; Flemings, like Rubens and Teniers; Dutchmen, including Steen and de Hooch; and Britons, including Reynolds and still another ducal portrait by Lawrence.

The Greenwich complex: Greenwich, southeast of London, first comes up in history as Placentia Palace, the very same in which Henry VIII lived and where his daughter, Queen Elizabeth I, was born. Later, during the reign of William and Mary, Sir Christopher Wren was commissioned by the Crown to design a naval hospital, now the *Royal Naval College*. Utilizing the position of the earlier Inigo Jones-designed *Queen's House*—inland from the Thames—as a focal point, Wren created two grand colonnades leading to and framing in the background the Queen's House and doubling as walls of the pair of domed blocks that constitute hospital-cum-college. Because the college remains very much in business, with midshipmen inhabiting it, its two great interiors traditionally may be seen only in the afternoon.

Worth seeing are the college's *Painted Hall* (with murals on walls and ceiling by Sir James Thornhill), which is now the midshipmen's dining room; and the *Chapel*, with a blue-and-gold ceiling and a celebrated painting of St. Paul, by Benjamin West, behind the altar.

Earlier-mentioned Queen's House is now but one of the three principal sectors of the *National Maritime Museum*, brimming with ships models and plans, navigational instruments, naval weapons and uniforms, and paintings of exceptional caliber. Personal favorites: Elizabeth I, by an unidentified genius; Charles I, by the studio of Daniel Luytens; Queen Henrietta Maria, by Van Dyck; Nelson, by L. F. Abbott; Lady Hamilton, by Romney.

There are other Greenwich attractions: Wren-designed Flamstead, the original *Royal Observatory* building, outside of which is the Greenwich Meridian-Longitude Zero, marked across the observatory's courtyard. Nearby is the venerable sailing vessel, *Cutty Sark* (the Scotch whisky was named for it, not vice versa). In Greenwich is a charmer of a church, *St. Alfege*, the work of Wren's assistant, Nicholas Hawksmoor, built during the reign of Queen Anne, who insisted that the church contain a royal pew. Lunch at the *Trafalgar Tavern* (Park Row), whose special lures are mementos of Lord Nelson.

Royal Academy of Arts (Burlington House, Piccadilly) is housed in a mid-nineteenth-century palazzo that has become a Piccadilly landmark. It's been staging annual summer shows for more than two centuries; there are, as well, special exhibits, which can be of extraordinary caliber.

Membership is selected through a complicated process. Sir Joshua Reynolds was the first president; Sir Christopher Wren was one of his successors. Not to be missed: the so-called Private Rooms, a suite of opulent galleries retained from earlier eighteenth-century Burlington House, with choice holdings from the Academy's own collection on view, including a sculpted Michelangelo *Madonna* and works by onetime members, including Reynolds, Gainsborough, and Turner.

Percival David Foundation of Chinese Art (53 Gordon Square), a unit of the University of London, is less celebrated than its sister-museum, the Courtauld Institute Galleries. Located in a Bloomsbury townhouse, this is a superlative display of Chinese treasures—porcelain, enamelware, and scrolls. All told, there are some 1,500 objects surveying Chinese art for the last millennium.

British Theatre Museum (Covent Garden): Drama buffs, in this most theater-rich of capitals, will find Siddons's Sheraton dressing table and letters, manuscripts, photos, and costumes galore—even one of Nijinsky's.

Dulwich College Picture Gallery (College Road) is a hike from central London, make no mistake. Give yourself half a day, and try to select a sunny one so that you can enjoy a stroll through this unlikely South London suburb with a still-bucolic air to its park-and-garden setting and its gem: the Sir John Soane-designed (1814) picture gallery—the first public one in London, a decade ahead of the National Gallery on Trafalgar Square. On display is a dazzling collection of Old Masters. The range is extraordinary— Lorrain and Poussin, Rembrandt and Cuyp, Rubens and Van Dyck, Canaletto and Murillo. There are fine English works, as well—Lelys, Knellers, Hogarths, Ramsays, and Gainsboroughs, among them. Not quite 40 of Dulwich's paintings crossed the Atlantic for the first time in 1986, to be shown at New York's National Academy of Design. But they're at their best on home ground. Go by train from Victoria Station.

Imperial War Museum (Lambeth Road): The empire is, of course, no more, but the Imperial War Museum stubbornly retains the name it has had since World War I days. You may or may not be attracted because of its associations with an empire that is extinct or because the theme is war or because the setting is the original mental hospital called by a name that has become part of the language: Bedlam. Still, the place may surprise you. What it sets out to do is show how the empire, oops, the Commonwealth, cooperated during the course of the two World Wars. The domed building is superb Regency, with a graceful portico. Galleries—navy, air, army—are chock-full of war objects, ranging from an actual German submarine to a French tank and a World War II Spitfire aircraft. Big surprise is the Picture Gallery; all of the works have war-related themes, and their creators include Sargent, Wyndham Lewis, Feliks Topolski, and Epstein.

Kenwood (Hampstead Heath), north of London and reachable by railway, is visitable as a great Robert Adam house (later counseled) and as a repository of paintings, these of the collection of brewer Edward Cecil Guinness, who bequeathed them, with the house, to the public in 1927. Kenwood constitutes a choice collection—both Gainsborough and Reynolds are heavily represented. So are Turner and Landseer, and so are the French, through Boucher and Watteau, and the Dutch, with Rembrandt and Vermeer.

Natural History Museum (Cromwell Road): Its absolute glory of a mock-Romanesque facade—two steeple-like towers over the entrance, a pair of square towers delineating its flanks—makes this the most architecturally distinguished of the South Kensington museums; even the next-door Victoria and Albert Museum pales in contrast. Architect Alfred Waterhouse's building was begun in 1873 and not completed until seven years later. The facade is esthetic reward enough. Go inside, then, to the Central Hall; you might well have entered a Romanesque cathedral on the Italian peninsula, except that this space has an added attraction—a suspended passageway at its extreme end that just has to be modeled on the Bridge of Sighs in Venice's Doges' Palace. Exhibits? Most spectacular is a staggeringly immense blue whale. But this is a world-class museum, with its range mammals and fossils, birds and fishes, insects and reptiles, rocks and minerals. And I should point out that, if my experience is typical, you and your party will be the only nonteacher adults in attendance; the masses of class groups are overwhelming enough for this place to be known also as the Museum of British Schoolchildren.

Science Museum (Exhibition Road): Not unlike counterparts in Chicago, Washington, and Munich, London's Science Museum is (a) enormous and (b) child-filled. But the kids can't be faulted, given exhibits like pioneering railway locomotives and equally early autos, antique clocks and tractors, early phonographs and cameras, and even mockups of Victorian kitchens and bathrooms. (If you've sufficient curiosity, visit also the neighboring *Geology Museum* [Exhibition Road], where you might enjoy sparkling displays of emeralds, rubies, sapphires, and diamonds.)

Commonwealth Institute (Kensington High Street at Holland Park): A post-World War II structure that looks as though it might have been displaced from a world's fair,

the institute is only partially a museum. It's a commendable enterprise designed to put the various Commonwealth countries' best feet forward to the people of the
United Kingdom. Its museum aspect embraces two vast
floors of exhibits—of each and every one of the Commonwealth countries. (Nigeria, in my view, is the don't-miss of
the lot.) Noteworthy, too, is an art gallery with frequently
changing shows of Commonwealth artists, often two or
three at a time.

London Transport Museum (Covent Garden) occupies
the massive and splendidly restored nineteenth-century
building that had for long housed Covent Garden's Flower
Market. If you're an aficionado of double-decker London
buses and the Underground (and what visitor to London is
not?), you're bound to have a good time here, traipsing
through historic predecessors of equipment now in use,
some of it—the very first Hackney coaches, for example—
going back two centuries. Delightful London Transport
posters, from over the years, are dotted about, along with
all manner of memorabilia, including staff uniforms of
yesteryear.

Madame Tussaud's (Marylebone Road): I dignify this establishment by including it in this section of selected museums only because you will have heard of it, and may
want to go. Well, unless you see them, you can't believe
how awful many of the wax statues are, particularly those
of the contemporary personalities whose faces we are familiar with from newspapers, films, and television.

MEMORIAL HOUSES

Thomas Carlyle's House (Cheyne Row, Chelsea) is small
and on a street of small houses. It's as good an excuse as
any to visit this good-looking Chelsea quarter—bordering

the Thames and with more substantial Cheyne (pronounced *cheyney*) Walk its most noted thoroughfare. The
house was more than a century old when Carlyle and his
wife moved in, in 1834, remaining until the author died in
1881. Furnishings are the Carlyles' own. To be seen are the
top-floor studio, living room, and bedroom and the basement kitchen.

Charles Dickens' House (Doughty Street) was Dickens'
home for only two years (1837–39), but the prolific author,
in that brief period, wrote *Oliver Twist* and *Nicholas
Nickleby* there and worked on other books, too. There's a
remarkably complete library of and about Dickens, as well
as a Pickwick-type kitchen below-stairs.

William Hogarth's House (Hogarth Lane, Chiswick):
Considering that it was badly damaged during World War
II and had to be restored, this house conveys a graphic picture of what it must have been when Hogarth and his wife
used it as a country retreat in the mid-eighteenth century.
There is precious little furniture, but there is a quantity of
the master's prints.

Dr. Samuel Johnson's House (Gough Square) is a four
story Queen Anne house on a square tucked behind Fleet
Street and is reached by the same alley on which the venerable Cheshire Cheese pub has its entrance. Johnson
chose it in order to be near the printer of his monumental
dictionary. He lived in the house between 1748 and 1759,
during which time the dictionary was a major project, with
half a dozen copyists working on it exclusively.

John Keats' House (Keats Grove, Hampstead) is early
nineteenth century, handsome, and full of mementos of
the gifted young poet, who was only twenty-five when he

died in Rome. Next door is a library full of editions of Keats's works and portraits of him.

SQUARES: A SUM-UP

Trafalgar Square is No. 1, with a landmark (170-foot-high Nelson pillar), playing water (the fountains are among London's loveliest), structures of note (National Gallery, St. Martin-in-the-Fields Church, nearby Charing Cross Railway Station), and the scenic view along Whitehall—to Big Ben and Parliament.

Piccadilly Circus, its relatively recently refurbished statue of Eros notwithstanding (originally unveiled in 1893), has all of the charm of New York's Times Square, which is to say, not much. Heaven knows, though, how many passengers throng its excellently run Underground station per day. And the Circus is central: theaterland east on Shaftesbury Avenue, Regent Street stores to the north, and Mayfair to the west via Piccadilly.

Soho Square remains partly eighteenth-century and has given its name to the multicultural foreign quarter adjacent to the theaters, with two churches, one French Protestant, the other (St. Patrick's) Catholic and—on Greek and Frith and adjacent streets—restaurants serving cuisines of Italy, France, Greece, China, Hungary, and India.

Grosvenor Square is important to North Americans. The former neo-Georgian American Embassy is now an annex of the Canadian High Commission, the Americans having moved to a striking Eero Saarinen-designed embassy, powerful, good-looking, and appropriate to the site, with an oversized eagle over the entrance that had London agog when it went up in 1960. Note, too, Sir William Reid Dick's statue of President Franklin D. Roosevelt, a British tribute to the close Anglo-American cooperation of the World War II era.

Belgrave Square is the epitome of elegant London, a Regency-era jewel, surrounded by fine houses, today sheltering embassies (Austrian, German, Japanese, Spanish) and scholarly societies. *Eaton, Cadogan,* and heavily American-populated *Chester* squares are nearby and similarly posh, and the area's streets—Wilton Crescent, Belgrave Place, Chesham Place, Pont Street—are, too.

Sloane Square is synonymous with Chelsea. King's Road leads both east and west from it. Sloane Street leads north to Knightsbridge, and Lower Sloane Street heads south toward Chelsea Embankment and the Thames.

Bloomsbury Square and its neighbors are dominated by the British Museum and the University of London. Exiting the museum, have a look at *Bedford, Russell,* and *Tavistock* squares and the quarter's streets.

PRETTIEST PARKS

St. James's and *Green* parks and *Buckingham Palace Gardens* are the most central of the parks and are contiguous. St. James's is bisected by a lake where birds breed. Green Park borders on Hyde (below), with Wellington Arch and Hyde Park Corner the points of contact between the two. *Hyde Park*'s spark is *Speaker's Corner*—what free speech in Britain is all about. But there are, as well, boating on the Serpentine, riding on Rotten Row, and band concerts at the Achilles Statue. *Kensington Gardens* is adjacent to Hyde Park, to its west. Originally Kensington Palace's front yard, it now draws small fry who will sail bathtub-size boats in the Round Pond. *Regent's Park's* big draw is *London Zoo*, with an aviary designed by Lord Snowdon and open-space confinement areas for big animals, as well as a reputed aquarium and, at the south end, the late Queen Mary's rose garden. *Kew Gardens* is officially the *Royal Botanic Gardens*, lovely to walk about (there are 25,000 botanic specimens), with a onetime royal residence—*Kew Palace*—an eminently inspectable retreat of no less a monarch than George III, whose consort, Queen Charlotte, died within, in 1818.

Hampstead Heath has two things going for it: *Kenwood House* (see above and below) and elevation—400 feet at its highest—that assures a smashing view of central London to the south. Relax at venerable *Spaniards Inn* pub (Spaniards Road); have a look at Georgian, village-like Hampstead adjacent.

PERIPHERAL LONDON: SELECTED COUNTRY HOUSES

Ham House (Richmond, Surrey) went up in the early seventeenth century. One enters a galleried Great Hall hung with paintings by Reynolds, Kneller, and Van Dyck, but that is only the beginning. Elsewhere you'll see textiles, plasterwork, wood carving, mantels, mirrors, wall coverings, parquet floors, painted ceilings, and furniture. There is not an inferior piece of work in the house.

Not to be missed: the Great Staircase; the Duchess's bedroom, with its immense, red-canopied bed; the upstairs Long Gallery, with its Sir Peter Lely paintings of voluptuous ladies; and the North Drawing Room, with its English tapestries, gilded chairs, and a marble fireplace banked by twisted half-columns. Café.

Chiswick House (Burlington Lane, Chiswick) is probably the greatest pure Palladian villa outside of the prototypes in the Veneto region of northern Italy. Chiswick was built in 1725 by Lord Burlington after his return from a Grand Tour on which he saw the originals. Chiswick was designed by William Kent—the multitalented landscapist-cabinetmaker-architect—in collaboration with Lord Burlington. It is smallish, and today it is largely unfurnished. But Kent's elaborate ceilings and wall decorations compensate for the lack of chairs, tables, sofas, rugs, and paintings. There are three exceptionally striking chambers: the Red Velvet Room, the Blue Velvet Room, and, loveliest of the lot, the Central Gallery in white and gold.

Osterley Park House (Great West Road, Middlesex) is the earliest of several Robert Adam-designed country houses in the London area. Adam's goal was "delicacy, gaiety, grace and beauty"—hardly immodest, but he attained it. Osterley's principal rooms are just as Adam created them, and that includes furniture he had especially made for each. The entrance hall stuns with its magnificence—a ballroom-size, high-ceilinged chamber, with the decoration consisting solely of the gray-and-white marble floor and the plasterwork on the walls and ceiling, in Wedgwood blue and white. There is a severely beautiful library, a dining room where a series of console tables placed against the walls (with the chairs) take the place of a conventional dining table; a Long Gallery with pale green walls to match the furniture in the same hue; and a room in which tapestries cover the walls, like elaborate wallpaper.

Syon House (Brentford, Middlesex) has never, in all of its four centuries-plus, altered its stern gray Tudor facade. Edward VI was the first of many celebrated visitors to enjoy Syon's hospitality. Lady Jane Grey, who reigned as

Queen for nine days before her beheading, was offered the crown at Syon. By the mid-eighteenth century, Syon had become the seat of the dukes of Northumberland. In 1762, the twelfth duke hired Robert Adam to transform the interior of Syon, while retaining the Tudor facade. The entrance hall, influenced by that at Osterley Park (above), is similar to it and painted in pale gray, the only other hue provided by the black tiles of a checkerboard marble floor. The Anteroom, with black marble pillars supporting gold neoclassic statues that in turn support a gilded ceiling, is an eye-opener. The Red Drawing Room is dazzling, and so is its art: painting after painting by Lely and Van Dyck. And the Long Gallery has books lining its pale green walls and an intricate Adam ceiling.

Kenwood House (Hampstead Lane, Hampstead) is the latest of our trio of London-area Adam-designed houses. Lord Mansfield, its then-owner, retained Adam in 1764 to transform an older house. Its State Room leads off an oblong entrance hall into two equally proportioned wings. Detailing is minute. The Library, with its arched ceiling supported by Corinthian columns, is the showplace room. Kenwood is also an art gallery of consequence (see Museumgoers London, this chapter).

Hatfield House (Hertfordshire): The present house's predecessor—still standing—was the royal palace in which Henry VIII's daughter, Bloody Mary, kept her younger half-sister, the Princess Elizabeth, prisoner during part of Mary's reign. It was at Hatfield—in the old palace that now serves as a restaurant—that Elizabeth learned of her accession to the throne. The newer—and main—house is a Jacobean manor built by the first Earl of Salisbury (whose descendants are still resident). Its two-story-high Great Hall—with one wall covered with a trio of Brussels tapestries and another with a carved wooden screen—is one of the superlative English rooms and is the locale of Hilliard's so-called ermine painting of Elizabeth I and the Oudry portrait of her adversary, Mary Queen of Scots. Hatfield abounds in fine rooms—King James Drawing Room, with its red and white ceiling and red and gold furniture; 180-foot-long Long Gallery; capacious library; and chapel.

Luton Hoo (Luton, Bedfordshire): Queen Elizabeth II and Prince Philip made it a habit, at least before the 1973 death of Sir Harold Wernher, to weekend at Luton Hoo. The house itself, begun by Robert Adam in 1767 and set in a Capability Brown-conceived park, stands behind a turn-of-century rose garden. Loveliest of the rooms are the eighteenth-century French Blue Hall and dining room, the latter equipped with crystal and silver that belonged to English monarchs and with Beauvais tapestries covering the walls. Art treasures embrace furniture, porcelain, sculpture, ivories, Renaissance jewelry, and extraordinary Old Master paintings, including works of Italians like Lippi and Flemings like Memling.

Woburn Abbey (Bedfordshire) is a pioneer in the Stately Home business. The 300-year-old house is treasure filled, with such splendid interiors as the drawing, dressing, and bedrooms in which Queen Victoria and Prince Albert stayed on their visits and the Long Gallery, with such paintings as the noted Armada portrait of Elizabeth I, a likeness of Elizabeth's half-sister Bloody Mary, after Sir Anthony More, and a Holbein of Jane Seymour. Owner-operator not only of the house, but of ancillary commercial enterprises is the Marquess of Tavistock. If you go by car, Woburn may be comfortably combined in a single day with Luton Hoo. A recommended lunch break would be at *Paris House,* a luxury-category French restaurant on the

Woburn estate, or at a venerable inn-restaurant called *The Bell*, in nearby Aston Clinton.

THE TEN TOP DAY-EXCURSIONS FROM LONDON

The point about day-excursions out of London is not to over-do them. It must be appreciated that they are a case of half a loaf being better than none. You don't get the Georgian flavor of Bath without a night or two there, affording time for casual strolls along its eighteenth-century streets. Canterbury is a substantial country town—more than its landmark cathedral. The Cotswolds exemplify British village life at its most charming; you want time to chat up postmistresses doubling as shopkeepers, publicans over leisurely beers—that kind of thing. Both Oxford and Cambridge are so extraordinarily rich in art and architecture that you simply skim the surface in the course of a day's outing. I make my case for the Britain beyond London in this book's companion volume, *Britain at Its Best*. At this point, let me counsel the following day-long outings from the capital for the time-short traveler. Order is alphabetical.

BATH

It was the Romans who made Bath a spa, naming it for still-therapeutic waters. Medieval Britons adorned it with perhaps the most sublimely proportioned of Britain's abbey churches. And then, in the early eighteenth century, a long-somnolent Bath reemerged into a Golden Age dazzler of a watering hole: architecturally stunning (credit the John Woods, Senior and Junior), socially the capital of the kingdom (credit unofficial ruler Beau Nash), intellectually absorbing (credit such house renters as Richard Brinsley Sheridan, William Wordsworth, Jane Austen, and Thomas Gainsborough), and politically potent (with settlers-in including George III's consort, Queen Charlotte; George IV's morganatic wife, Mrs. Fitzherbert; William Pitt; and Lord Nelson).

Bath's ravishing squares and crescents serve as landmarks as one proceeds from the core of town: *Bath Abbey* and the neighboring *Roman Baths.* High Street is just north of the Abbey. A classic walk would take you across the Robert Adam-designed, shop-lined *Pulteney Bridge,* over the River Avon, and on to mansion-lined Great Pulteney Street, at whose end is the colonnaded facade of the first-rate *Holbourne of Menstrie Museum,* with paintings by Gainsborough, Romney, Ramsay, Stubbs, and even Gilbert Stuart; as well as fine Georgian furniture.

Another walk would take you from the Abbey north along Union and Milson streets' smart shops, with a turn west to George Street; thence north on Gay Street to *The Circus*—lined by classic houses—and due west via Brock Street to *Royal Crescent,* the masterwork of the architect Woods, father and son, comprising no less than 30 joined mansions united by a series of Ionic columns, 114, all told. *Landsdown Crescent,* farther north and elevated so as to afford a panorama of the city, is lovely, too. Have lunch at the extraordinarily beautiful *Royal Crescent Hotel* (Royal Crescent), *Popjoy's* (Sawclose), *Hole in the Wall* (George Street), or the *Priory Hotel* (Weston Road).

BRIGHTON

Brighton stands out among south coast resorts for two good reasons. Location is one—London is less than an hour's ride north, with trains departing hourly. And a strong royal association is the other. King George IV, while he was Prince Regent in the closing decades of the eighteenth century, selected Brighton as the site of a pleasure palace that put it on the visitors' map—apparently for all time. He was so taken with the place on a visit in 1783 that he bought a small house, on the site of which he erected the first Royal Pavilion in mock-classic style. Not long thereafter, he hired architect John Nash, who designed an Indo-Chinese pavilion around the earlier house, and, before long, Brighton became a fashionable resort.

Not unlike its builder, the *Royal Pavilion* (Castle Square) is extravagant and impractical, but with a splendid sense of style and drama—a veritable Mogul palace embracing plump towers, slim minarets, intricately detailed arches without, and outrageously exaggerated Indo-Chinese within. Note the exquisite design details.

Furniture, wallpaper, carpets, textiles, walls and ceilings, pillars and chandeliers—all are of a caliber to have impelled exportation of a generous sampling across the Atlantic for a 1977 exhibition at the Cooper Hewitt Museum, the Smithsonian Institution's branch in New York. You'll enjoy bamboo-accented corridors, a grandiose banqueting room, a kitchen with a ceiling supported by amusing fake palm trees, music and drawing rooms, and the suite created for the Prince when he finally—at the age of 58—ascended the throne. The Prince Regent's morganatic wife, Mrs. Fitzherbert, built a house (today it's the YMCA), and others of the Prince's retinue became residents.

Take time for the *Brighton Art Gallery and Museum* (Church Street)—originally the Prince Regent's stables, with a Sir Thomas Lawrence portrait of "Prinnie" in coronation robes, upon becoming George IV, among its works, the range, William Hogarth to Salvador Dalí. Stroll *The Lanes*—a quarter of pre-Regency streets deftly refurbished as a venue for antique and other shops. And consider lunch at *Le Grandgousier* (15 Western Street—and French) or *Wheeler's* (The Lanes—for seafood).

CAMBRIDGE

Cambridge can attribute its eminence as seat of one of the

world's great universities to another university—Oxford (below). What happened, in the early thirteenth century, was that a group of students at Oxford felt it expedient to get out of town after authorities had hanged some classmates on charges of murder. The migrant Oxonians settled in Cambridge and in little more than a decade had founded their own university in what had been an obscure east-central market town on the River Cam. Cambridge University—not unlike older and, to my mind, less beautiful, somewhat scruffy-appearing Oxford—spreads itself around the core of the city whose name it takes.

It embraces a central administration that's an umbrella for 31 colleges, each with its own cluster of buildings— garden flanked and courtyard centered and often of considerable architectural distinction. Peterhouse, the oldest college, opened in 1284; Churchill, the newest, dates only to 1959. Pick up a map at the Cambridge Tourist Information Centre (Wheeler Street), concentrating your tour on this selection of colleges: *Corpus Christi* (Trumpington Street), with a treasure-filled library; *Emmanuel* (St. Andrew's Street)—with a Sir Christopher Wren-designed Baroque chapel, within which is a plaque honoring alumnus John Harvard; *Christ's* (St. Andrew's Street)—with the rooms believed to have been those of poet John Milton when he was a student; *St. John's* (St. John's Street)—with a Bridge of Sighs spanning the River Cam and a painting-filled dining hall; *Magdalene* (Magdalene Street)—with a collection of books in its library given by seventeenth-century diarist Samuel Pepys; *Trinity* (Trinity Street)— with a fine Gothic chapel and a dining hall portrait by Holbein of Henry VIII, the college's founder; and *King's* (King's Parade)—whose Gothic chapel, with fan vaulting extending the length of its 289-foot ceiling, is Cambridge's principal visitor lure. Pause for lunch in the excellent café of *Fitzwilliam Museum* (Trumpington Street), reserving the afternoon for the museum's splendid paintings—the range, Brueghel and Titian, Lorrain and Veronese, Rembrandt and Van Dyck, Pissarro and Renoir, Hogarth and Turner.

CANTERBURY

Canterbury, though tucked away in England's southeast corner, is not what you would call isolated. Roman troops invaded in the first century; in the sixth, St. Augustine converted the King of Kent to Christianity; in the twelfth, four knights—acting for King Henry II—murdered Archbishop Thomas Becket in his own cathedral; and in the sixteenth, Henry VIII, leading a resplendent fleet, sailed from nearby Dover to meet with France's King François I on the Field of Cloth of Gold.

Fronted by High Street in a town center delightfully weathered and evocative of past centuries, *Canterbury Cathedral*—as seat of the Archbishop of Canterbury, Primate of All England—is the kingdom's single most important church. It embraces a meld of styles and centuries, early Norman (its western crypt) through Victorian Gothic (its northwest tower). To many, its quite literally crowning achievement is its central—or "Bell Harry"—tower, whose 235-foot height dominates the town. Inside, the nave overwhelms in a space that is an indisputably outstanding specimen of Perpendicular, the third and final of the three English Gothic periods. Note the fan vaulting of the interior central tower; the immense choir; the steps worn by centuries, aptly called Pilgrim steps, that lead to Trinity Chapel, for long the location of St. Thomas Becket's tomb; the stone tablet marking the spot where Becket was murdered; and the parts of the cathedral that are to me the most beautiful: a tranquil cloister and a pair of Romanesque chapels in the crypt.

Two museums tell Canterbury's story—*Westgate* (St. Peter's Street), occupying an ancient city gate; and *Royal* (High Street), Victorian-era and art filled. Have lunch at

Sully's (County Hotel, High Street) or, if you've a car, at *Eastwell Manor Hotel* in nearby Ashford. If there's time in the afternoon, visit the neighboring town of *Rochester,* whose lures are somber, albeit lovely, *Rochester Cathedral* (it goes back a thousand years and melds Romanesque with Early English Gothic) and *Eastgate House* (High Street), an aged house, now a museum, with interesting Dickens associations.

THE COTSWOLDS

The Cotswolds are a cluster of too-good-to-be-true villages that constitute a southwest-to-northeast diagonal between Bath (above) and Stratford-upon-Avon (below). Their name comes from the network of gently rolling hills in which they're set. They have been built of beige sandstone, locally quarried, and, quite obviously, of considerable staying power. You go not for intellectual stimulation, but rather for relaxation. These villages are largely one-street affairs, invariably with a charming church of respectable vintage (not always open), an inn or two or three, a choice of places of sustenance, and, it should go without saying, a plethora of shops, along with the occasional unassuming little museum of local lore.

I am partial to the villages in the northern part of the region not only because of their smashing good looks (each could be a Ye Olde England movie set), but also for strategic considerations. You may reach them easily by train from London (board at Paddington station, exit at Moreton-in-Marsh, where you may hire a car). Though tiny, *Broadway* is not without monuments. The tower that takes its name —nineteenth-century mock-Gothic— affords smashing views from its summit. St. Edburghas Church dates back a thousand years. The adjacent village of *Stanton* is a Cotswolds microcosm: stone farmhouses and barns in sheep-populated meadows edging it, with a stunner of a Gothic church in its center. Still another near-to-Broadway village, *Stowshill*, boasts Stowshill Manor, a Tudor-era house-museum.

Chipping Campden's Woolstaplers Hall Museum dates to 1340 and brims with local historical exhibits. A row of severe stone almshouses leads to the Perpendicular Gothic tower of the big parish church. The fifteenth-century Market Hall is outstanding, too. At *Moreton-in-Marsh*, the venerable Market Hall is a High Street landmark. There's an oddball Curfew Tower topped with a four-century-old curfew bell, and a gracefully steepled parish church.

Have lunch in the *Lygon Arms Hotel's* ranker of a restaurant (Broadway), that same hotel's *Goblets Wine Bar*, at Chipping Campden's *Noel Arms Hotel*, or at Moreton-in-Marsh's *Manor House Hotel*.

OXFORD

Oxford, though less bucolic and less well manicured than Cambridge (above), is hardly without its share of historic, architectural, and intellectual distinction. Its university—older than Cambridge—is a consequence of a trickle of students who came from Paris, of all places, in the early twelfth century, when England's King Henry II recalled those of his countrymen studying in France. Before long, they had set up a system of halls—centers for both teaching and boarding—each directed by an alumnus. And so the pioneering Oxford system of the residential college evolved. The university is a confederation of 28 undergraduate colleges and seven postgraduate colleges, each with its own enclosed campus, library, dorms, and dining halls, which share the common university facilities—museums, science labs, and libraries. The major concentration of colleges is in the vicinity of High Street as it proceeds eastward from the busy city center. Ask for a map at the Oxford Tourist Information Centre (St. Aldate's

Street), concentrating on a representative sprinkling of colleges, to fill your morning. Most time-consuming—it is a triple-threat, admission-charging college-chapel/ cathedral-art museum—is *Christ College* (St. Aldate's Street). Landmark Tom Tower, over its main gate, was designed by Sir Christopher Wren. Walk through it to the immense dining hall, its walls lined with good paintings. Proceed, then, to the college chapel that is, as well, Oxford Cathedral (the dean of the cathedral serves also as head of Christ College), like no other in Britain, with its nave lined by chunky columns that are Romanesque at their base, but with Corinthian capitals, and with its choir covered by a later ceiling, the ribs of whose vaults are star shaped. End in Christ's sleeper of a Picture Gallery, with a small but rich collection, mostly Italian, and including Lippi, Tintoretto, Veronese, Carracci, Strozzi, and Rosa, with a bonus of drawings by the likes of Lorrain, Raphael, Titian, and Dürer.

All Souls (High Street) had Henry VI as a cofounder six centuries ago. Its twin towers are an Oxford landmark, a Wren protégé designed its splendid main quadrangle; its library has a Wren-wrought sundial; and its chapel—soaring Perpendicular Gothic—has a brilliant high altar and carved-wood choir. *New College* (New College Lane) was new in 1379, when William of Wykeham, bishop of Winchester (below) established it. Aside from a Sir Jacob Epstein sculpture of Lazarus at the chapel entrance, it is almost completely the Gothic college of Wykeham's day, with linenfold wood paneling (characterized by a pattern of close-together vertical slits) in its dining hall and chapel art that includes windows painted by Reynolds and an El Greco near the altar.

Break for lunch in the *Randolph Hotel* (Beaumont Street). Just opposite is the university-operated *Ashmolean Museum*, easily on a par with Cambridge's Fitzwilliam (above). Start on the main floor, with finds from Roman

Britain, Egypt, and ancient Greece. Ascend to upper floors, then, for stars of the show: paintings by such Italians as Bellini, Michelangelo, Veronese, Raphael, and Bronzino; such Low Countries greats as Van Dyck, Rubens, and Rembrandt; with Lorrain, Watteau, and Chardin, among the French; and Hogarth, Constable, and Gainsborough, among the English; all of the leading Impressionists—Cézanne and Monet, Van Gogh and Renoir, Manet and Pissarro; and beyond to Bonnard and Picasso. The university's *Bodleian Library* (Broad Street) displays priceless illuminated manuscripts. And you want to pop into the Wren-designed *Sheldonian Theatre* (Broad Street) to see its spectacular painted ceiling.

ST. ALBANS

St. Albans is a small town with a big cathedral. When the Romans ruled 2,000 years back, it was called *Verulamium*, and among the townspeople was a soldier named Alban who, legend has it, was executed by the anti-Christian authorities in the course of protecting a priest. The Saxon church where the sainted Alban was killed has long since been replaced by what is now *St. Alban's Cathedral*, a Romanesque-Gothic meld with a narrow nave that, at 300 feet, is among the world's longest. The saint's shrine is what one wants to see first, along with the intricately carved choir, sculpted saints of the altar screen, and painted saints on walls and ceilings. Nearby *Verulamium Museum* shelters remnants of Roman St. Albans, beautiful mosaics most especially. Lunch at the *White Hart* (Holywell Hill), a pub mellowed by age; it's twelfth century.

SALISBURY

Salisbury: If a single place name conjures up the prototype of the English cathedral town, it is southerly Salisbury. An early nineteenth-century painter who wandered south from East Anglia—John Constable, by name—to paint its cathedral is largely responsible for this state of affairs. All the world appears to know the Constable oils of the single-pinnacle church, cows grazing contentedly on the banks of the River Avon, out back. The livestock has, to be sure, disappeared; but if Constable were to return today, he could paint *Salisbury Cathedral* quite as he had originally. Dating to the early thirteenth century, its 404-foot spire—loftiest such in England—has no vertical competition. And from every direction—looking east from the square of emerald lawn in the massive cloister, north from the bucolic banks of the Avon, west from across the expanse of The Close, or lawn—the cathedral is serenely beautiful. Your first impression—looking down the very long, unobstructed nave—is of architecture that is immediately understandable. As you walk about, note the bishop's throne above the choir; octagonal Chapter House, fan vaulted; even a copy of *Magna Carta*—one of four—in the Morning Chapel. The *Salisbury & South Wiltshire Museum* (The Close) occupies a superb stone mansion of yore, and is treasure filled. Two neighboring houses on The Close—*Monpesson* (dating to 1701) and *Malmesbury* (even older)—are furnished in period and welcome visitors. *Wilton House*, three miles west of town, is one of Britain's great country mansions; its Double Cube Room is so named because it is exactly twice as long as it is wide, and its walls are lined with Van Dyck paintings. Wilton has a pair of restaurants, where you might have lunch, considering *Haunch of Venison* (Minster Street) or *Provençal* (Market Place) as in-Salisbury alternatives.

Stratford-upon-Avon

Stratford-upon-Avon's sole industry is trading upon its having been—some four centuries back—the town in which William Shakespeare was born. Countless visitors, many of whom have doubtless never read Shakespeare nor seen his works performed, stream into this riverside town some 80 miles northwest of London to pay, quite literally, their respects to the Bard's memory. They stream in and out of a handful of restored Tudor houses with Shakespeare associations, usually leaving at the end of the day, too early to take in a performance at the theater where his works are performed and which, when all is said and done, is Stratford at its most worthwhile.

If you're going to go to what is, as far as I can tell from my explorations, Britain's only tourist-trap town (even the church in which Shakespeare is buried charges a fee to see his tomb), do book a hotel room (choice is excellent in Stratford) so that you can see a performance at the *Royal Shakespeare Theatre*, overlooking the swan-populated Avon, as it flows through the heart of town, constituting Stratford's only concession to charm, and parallel to the main street, variously called High, Chapel, and Church.

The so-called Shakespearian properties are operated by an enterprise called the Shakespeare Birthplace Trust. *New Place* (Chapel Street) is not New Place, the house in which Shakespeare lived his last years (and died), but rather a house next door to New Place, whose foundation can be seen in the adjacent—and wonder of wonders in Stratford—open-for-free garden. The structure now identified as New Place is actually a museum of Stratford history (ideally, that is what it should be called), with some excellent Elizabethan furniture and exhibits relating to the town's past.

Shakespeare's Birthplace (Henley Street) embraces a living room, kitchen, and bedrooms—including the room in which the playwright was born—with the only original piece the desk he is believed to have used at school. *Hall's Croft* (Old Town) is the onetime residence of the physician who married Shakespeare's daughter, Susanna; its rooms include a dispensary. *Anne Hathaway's Cottage* (a mile to the west of Shottery) is thatch roofed, its carved four-poster bed the standout in its interior. You do not need to be reminded that Anne (eight years her husband's senior) became Mrs. Shakespeare; the year was 1582. *Holy Trinity Church* (Trinity Street) lies alongside the Avon. Its huge Perpendicular Gothic windows impress, as does its beamed ceiling. A verger, sitting at a cash desk at the high altar and selling tickets to see Shakespeare's tomb, is something else again. If you can, drive out to *Ragley Hall* (eight miles west of Stratford)—an exquisitely furnished eighteenth-century mansion whose 70-foot-long Great Hall, created by James Gibbs, with Gibbs's plaster decorations picked out in pale gray against a salmon background, is not misnamed. Have lunch in either of Stratford's oldest hotels, each handsome—the *Shakespeare* (Chapel Street) or the *Alveston Manor* (Clopton Bridge), the more interesting of the pair.

WINCHESTER

Winchester—a near-neighbor of Salisbury (above), which can be worked in with it, in the course of a *very* long, tightly organized day   goes back to the ninth-century reign of King Alfred, when it was capital of England, called Wessex at the time, remaining so until after the Norman Conquest in the eleventh century. *Winchester Cathedral*, not far from central High Street, is the third on the site and opened within decades of William the Conqueror's accession in 1066. That Romanesque structure remains in part. But Winchester's glory is the scale it achieves in the Perpendicular Gothic reconstruction brought to conclusion under the creative bishopric of William of Wykeham (see Oxford, above). You want to inspect the twelfth-century *Winchester Bible* and the charter presented to the cathedral by Henry VIII when it became Anglican, in the library, and ancient frescoes in the Holy Sepulchre Chapel. Don't fail to survey the nave from the west entrance; it is one of the longest and loveliest in Christendom. Dead ahead will be the high altar. It is backed by a reredos in whose niches are a score of sculpted saints, the lot surrounding a sublime *Crucifixion.* For me, there is no more beautiful cathedral.

But there's more in Winchester—what is believed to be King Arthur's Round Table in the Great Hall, all that remains of medieval *Winchester Castle* (High Street); the also-medieval complex of *Winchester College* (College Street), Wykeham-founded and one of England's premier public schools; the twelfth-century *Hospital of St. Cross* (St. Cross Road), housing a dozen each poor and titled gents of advanced age—each with distinctive robes—quite as it has since 1136; and *Winchester City Museum* (The Square) —with an intact mosaic floor from Roman Winchester its single most handsome exhibit. Have lunch in the *Wessex Hotel* (Paternoster Row, opposite the cathedral) or, if you've wheels, at *Lainston House Hotel,* at Sparsholt, just beyond town.

3

London To Watch

THE CAPITAL AFTER DARK

Sitting back—more often than not, sitting forward—and watching or listening is a diversion at which London is equaled for virtuosity and variety only by New York and Paris.

Theater in this No. 1 Theater City of the World comes first with most visitors, as with so many Londoners and provincial Britons—so much so that it tends, at least with newcomers, to overshadow the musical life of the capital, which is one of the richest on the planet.

This is, as well, a major ballet center, with opera nearly as celebrated. Britain remains a major cinema-producing nation, and London offers visitors a chance to see films not exported abroad—not to mention TV serializations of novels, plays, and historic events, only a fraction of which appear on American home screens.

Gambling is legal throughout Britain, with the consequence that London is one of the very few major world capitals with smart casinos at hand. Spectator sports run an expectedly wide gamut—limited by no means only to traditionally British cricket, soccer, and tennis.

SETTING THE STAGE

Theater in London goes back to the sixteenth century, when the first public theater opened in Shoreditch. Its impresario was James Burbage, who came to be the employer of William Shakespeare when the Bard left Stratford to become an actor in the capital. Within a couple of decades, the same Burbage opened a new theater on the Thames's south bank—the circular Globe that achieved immortality; the London theater tradition had become entrenched.

Today, the capital has more than half a hundred theaters, one of which—*Theatre Royal, Drury Lane*—is on the site of a predecessor that opened under Charles II's patronage three centuries ago. The Drury Lane is set behind an imposing neoclassic entrance portico. *Theatre Royal, Haymarket*, is another similarly aged, similarly atmospheric, and somewhat similarly porticoed beauty, its origin dating to the reign of George I, with its current home substantially the refurbishing of the Regent's John Nash. I am fond, too, of the *Royal Opera House, Covent Garden*. It is mid-nineteenth century, at once a place of splendor but still with an intimacy rarely found in opera houses on the Continent. And mind, I say this despite the decidedly regal aspects of the theater, including a royal box that has its own private supper room. A personal favorite, too, is the Edwardian *Coliseum*, home to the English National Opera, which has pioneered in the presentation of grand opera sung in the English language.

Most London theaters show productions especially produced and cast for a single run. But London has several repertory companies. The *National Theatre*, for long also called the Old Vic because its home was in the theater of that name, is the most noted (earlier members of its company included Dame Edith Evans, Sir Laurence Olivier, Vivien Leigh, Sir John Gielgud, Charles Laughton, and Sir

Alec Guinness—to name a few). Its home is a boldly handsome three-auditorium theater on the South Bank of the
Thames, a stellar specimen of British contemporary architecture. There is, as well, the *Royal Shakespeare Company.*
Its home base is the Royal Shakespeare Theatre in
Stratford, but it has for some time played London seasons,
as well, moving in 1982—when it opened—to the
revolutionary-design, 1,200-seat theater of the Barbican
Centre for Arts and Conferences in the Barbican quarter of
the City. The *Royal Court Theatre*, on Sloane Square in
Chelsea, is highly respected for an innovative policy that
has brought such playwrights as John Osborne (originally
with *Look Back in Anger)* to public attention. Much earlier, a
number of Shaw's plays were first seen at the Royal Court.

Glyndebourne Festival is English eccentricity carried to its
zenith and with great success over a period of two decades
in the form of top-rank opera (generally five works per
season), to the accompaniment of the London Philharmonic, at a country house 54 miles south of London, with
the prescribed dress black tie (men can get away with dark
suits). Glyndebourne's clincher is a 75-minute intermis-
sion to allow the formally dressed audience to picnic on
the lawns or to dine in a more prosaic on-premises restaurant. Season is late May through mid August, with many
customers transported by a special opera train that traditionally departs from London's Victoria Station at 2:55 P.M.
Harrods department store sells specially prepared picnic
packs, or order a hamper from caterers near Glyndebourne. Information and advance booking: Glyndebourne Festival, Lewes, England.

THE ROYAL OPERA AND
THE ROYAL BALLET

If London holds its own with the Royal Opera (whose repertory ranges from Verdi's *Il Trovatore* and Gounod's *Faust*

to Wagner's *The Flying Dutchman* and Richard Strauss's *Salome*, and whose patron is the Prince of Wales), it distinguishes itself with ballet. The Royal Ballet (whose patron is Princess Margaret) was born as the dance wing for the opera company originally associated with the Old Vic Theatre. When, with the advent of the thirties, the Sadler's Wells Theatre opened, the ballet took the name of the theater and under the direction of Ninette de Valois—later awarded the title "Dame" in recognition of her achievement—began to achieve international celebrity, to the point where it was honored by being given a permanent home just after World War II in the *Royal Opera House* (Covent Garden—with box office/shop in a detached, nearby building at 48 Floral Street, traditionally open from 10:00 A.M. to 8:00 P.M., Monday–Saturday). Another name change—to Royal Ballet—came not long thereafter. Frederick Ashton, later knighted for his work with the company, joined Dame Ninette as the company's principal choreographer in 1935, to be succeeded by Sir Kenneth MacMillan.

All three of these balletic giants shaped the company. The de Valois beginnings were essentially classical. Ashton carried on with that tradition (a Royal Ballet *Giselle* or *Swan Lake* is to this day a major London treat) and added his own imprint with such works as the dramatic *Daphnis and Chloe, Lady of the Camellias* (his interpretation of *Camille*), the lilting *Les Patineurs*, and the exuberant *Jazz Calendar*. MacMillan's major works have included a full-length *Romeo and Juliet* to music by Prokofiev, a balletic retelling of the Anastasia story, and his own interpretation of Stravinsky's *The Rite of Spring*. Recent years have seen the company take the works of contemporary foreign choreographers into the repertory, including New York City Ballet's George Balanchine (*Agon*) and Jerome Robbins (*Dances at a Gathering*). The company has an auxiliary wing, *The Royal Ballet New Group*. And there is other ballet—*Ballet Rambert, London Festival Ballet*—under the artistic direction of ex-Royal Danish Ballet soloist Peter Schaufuss; *London Contemporary Dance Theatre;* and *Sadler's Wells Royal Ballet,* headquartered in the original Sadler's Wells Theatre (Rosebery Avenue).

CONCERTS AND RECITALS

London has no fewer than five symphony orchestras. The *Royal Philharmonic,* founded in 1813, has its home base in Royal Festival Hall and never gives a concert without a bust of Beethoven on the stage. Beethoven wrote his Ninth Symphony for the orchestra and had close associations with it, as did such composers as Mendelssohn, who wrote his Fourth for the Royal Philharmonic, and Dvorak, who did likewise with his Second. The *London Symphony* is even older than the Royal Philharmonic. The *London Philharmonic,* founded by the late Sir Thomas Beecham, has in recent seasons been under the direction of Klaus Tennstädt; its home also is Royal Festival Hall. And there are, as well, the *BBC Symphony* and the *Philharmonia,* not to mention numerous chamber music groups, from the *London Mozart Players* to the *London Sinfonietta,* and symphonies from elsewhere in Britain. *Royal Liverpool Philharmonic, City of Birmingham Symphony,* and *Bournemouth Symphony,* to name but three, make London appearances along with orchestras from abroad.

Royal Festival Hall was built for the 1951 Festival of Britain on the South Bank of the Thames, near Waterloo Bridge. It is an absolutely super building, early-fifties contemporary at its very sensible, functional best, of reinforced concrete, with superb acoustics. The river setting is taken advantage of with a vast terrace affording fine vistas and above it a glass-walled restaurant. The auditorium seats 3,000. Adjacent, as part of the *South Bank Arts Centre,* are the smaller, also-attractive *Queen Elizabeth Hall* (1,100 seats) and the 370-seat *Purcell Room,* for chamber music. There is, as well, the *Hayward Gallery,* at which short-term art exhibits are held.

In contrast is *Royal Albert Hall,* in Kensington, built a century ago, named for the consort of Queen Victoria and just across the road from the elaborately sculpted memorial to him. The Royal Albert, unlike the Royal Festival, has never been loved for its acoustics. It has other things going for it, namely a capacity to seat 8,000 souls and a thousand-voice choir, all at once. Its organ is one of the biggest extant. The shape is circular—Royal Albert can be likened to a kind of fat silo.

London's newest concert venue—seating 2,000 and home base for the venerable London Symphony—is *Barbican Hall,* a part of the Barbican Centre for Arts and Conferences, a boldly designed, $265-million complex in the City's Barbican quarter, which opened in 1982.

Chamber music concerts and recitals are given regularly in *Wigmore Hall* (Wigmore Street). London's beautiful *churches* are frequent settings for musical events—*St. John's,* Smith Square, and *St. Martin-in-the-Fields,* on Trafalgar Square, are but two. Many, particularly in the City, give free lunchtime concerts. And in summer, at least when the weather cooperates, there are *outdoor musical events* at such locales as Holland Park, Victoria Embankment Gardens, and the Orangery of Kenwood House, Hampstead.

Booking theater, opera, and ballet tickets: There are few problems here, with the exception of concerts, particularly those of symphony orchestras in Royal Festival Hall and certain performances of the Royal Ballet and Royal Opera. The foregoing can be difficult to get seats for. Legitimate theater is usually easier. In all cases, the most direct and cheapest way of booking is in person at the theater box-office; many accept major credit cards. If this is inconvenient, there are the booking agencies, which add a service charge to the cost of each ticket; giant of the ticket-agency industry is Keith Prowse, whose head office is at Banda House, Cambridge Grove, London W6 OLE, and from whose U.S. branch (234 West 44th Street, New York, NY 10036; phone 1-800-223-4446) you may purchase tickets before you leave home. And every hotel of any size has a theater-booking cubbyhole. All of these establishments have supplies of weekly schedules of what's on in the theater, gratis. The daily press has the same information. *Leicester Square Ticket Booth* (Leicester Square) sells tickets for certain plays at half-price, plus a moderate service charge, on the day of performance; its usual hours are noon to 2:00 P.M. for matinee tickets, 2:30–6:30 P.M. for evening seats.

TRADITIONAL PAGEANTRY

Trooping the Colour marks the sovereign's birthday and takes place on an early June Saturday at Horse Guards Parade. The Queen is star of the show, mounted atop a royal horse. Prince Philip also participates, as do various units of the Royal Guard.

Royal Tournament is an annual event at Earl's Court, an immense arena-exhibition hall; entrants are members of the armed forces, and the show is at once music, derring-do, and pageantry.

State Opening of Parliament takes place early in November and embraces a procession beginning at Buckingham Palace and proceeding via The Mall, Horse Guards Parade, and Whitehall to the House of Lords, where the Queen reads her speech from the throne.

Order of the Garter Ceremony is an annual June event at Windsor Castle, with the Queen leading a resplendent procession from the castle proper to St. George's Chapel.

City of London Lord Mayor's Procession takes place the second Saturday in November. The Lord Mayor rides in his ancient coach from Guildhall to the Law Courts, where the Lord Chief Justice welcomes him.

SPECTATOR SPORTS

Cricket: Lords, in St. John's Wood, usually beginning in April and running into September.

Tennis: Wimbledon Championships are annual early-summer events at Wimbledon's Lawn Tennis and Croquet Club.

Racing: To be seen at Ascot, with dressy Royal Meetings à la *My Fair Lady*, is a June highlight; and Epsom, July and August.

Rowing: The Henley Royal Regatta is an annual early-July event at the Thames-side town of Henley, not far from London.

Horseback riding: The Royal International Horse Show at Wembley is an annual late-July event—show jumping is the highlight, and the Queen, herself a skilled equestrienne, often attends.

Croquet: The Croquet Association Open Championships, with teams from abroad competing in this very English and very ancient sport, take place at the Hurlingham Club.

Polo is played at a number of clubs, including the Guards Polo Club, Windsor, and the Ham Polo Club, Surrey.

CASINOS

There are a number of London casinos. The catch is that they are operated as private clubs, and only members may play. For a foreigner to be able to gamble, he or she must have been a member at least 48 hours—according to British law. So if you are interested, apply at one of the clubs *two days* before you plan to play; *take your passport with you* and be prepared to pay a membership fee. Casinos include the *21 Club* and that occupying the opulent, onetime ballroom (now with its own restaurant and bar) at the *Ritz Hotel* (Piccadilly).

4

London To Stay

SETTING THE HOTEL SCENE

First, let me say that I have lived in, dined in, and/or thoroughly inspected the hotels carefully selected for evaluation in these pages; they are divided into three price groups: *Luxury, First Class,* and *Moderate.* And let me say, too, that when a London hotel is running beautifully, there is none better. Service is gracious, everything will look good and work perfectly. It is, perhaps, worth bearing in mind that the better, older London hotels have had considerable experience in catering to Britain's upper classes and peerage—and there is no more knowing or demanding a clientele.

It is important to note, too, that London leads the kingdom in the maintenance, upgrading, modernization, and expansion of its hotel plant. Go back only a couple of decades to when Hilton International pioneered as the first foreign-based hotel chain to enter the London scene and compare its cosmopolitan composition today—with Inter-Continental, Sheraton, Regent International, Marriott, and Holiday Inns all represented. And with the management teams and staffs of even the British chains—the Savoy Group, for example, Trusthouse Forte, Prestige Hotels, Gleneagles Hotels, Rank Hotels, Thistle Hotels, Crest Hotels—you have a melting pot of nationalities. Time was—and not too far back—when a non-British hotel manager raised eyebrows. Today, he (or she) may be Spanish or German, Italian or French. At the same time, tables have been turned in the catering area, with skilled British chefs now commonplace, the while their colleagues in other departments are a veritable mini-UN—the range, Chinese and Scots, Indians and Yanks, Jamaicans and Greeks. And by and large, it works very well, indeed.

A WORD ABOUT BATHS

Baths—private ones, that is, in hotels—can be a sometime thing in Britain, even as we approach the twenty-first century. Luxury and first-class category hotels have them either in toto or almost completely. But in lower-category hotels, they can be rare. Baths with showers, in all except the newest hotels (especially outside London) are even rarer; and that includes the hand-operated "spritz" showers attached to tubs, a commonplace in hotel bathrooms of continental Europe. I make a point of trying to advise on these matters on pages following. Note, too, that washbasins with taps that mix hot and cold water are usually to be found in top-category London hotels, rarely in others. *With respect to hotels in this book, please note that all rooms have bath, unless otherwise noted.*

SELECTED LUXURY HOTELS

Athenaeum Hotel (116 Piccadilly; phone 499-3464) is a pre-World War II house, splendidly situated and small enough (112 smartly decorated rooms and suites) to be able to offer relatively personal service. The paneled bar is inviting; the restaurant—in pastel greens and pinks—likewise; and the long, sculpture-embellished lounge, pleasant for tea. A Rank hotel.

Berkeley Hotel (Wilton Place, off Knightsbridge; phone 235-6000) is the relatively modern successor to an earlier hotel of the same name, at another location. The facade is restrained and unadorned. Interiors are a mix of the contemporary with the traditional, employing marble, crystal, and antique paneling. The Berkeley (pronounced Barkeley) is not large—159 rooms and suites with exceptional baths. There are a pair of top-rank restaurants (the Buttery's buffet lunches are detailed on another page, while the main dining room's fare is more formal French), congenial drinking spaces, and an unexpected indoor swimming pool-cum-sauna on the roof. Lovely service. Member, Leading Hotels of the World.

Britannia Inter-Continental Hotel (Grosvenor Square; phone 629-9400): I had been an enthusiast of the Britannia even before Inter–Continental took it over and, with an £8 million budget, thoroughly and tastefully refurbished it. With its handsomely colonnaded, Georgian style facade on one of London's legendary squares, this elegantly traditional-style house has both location and looks in its favor—capacious lobby, Anglo-American cuisine in its Best of Both Worlds Restaurant (later evaluated), Waterloo Dispatch pub, classy Pine Bar, Japanese restaurant, and 437 rooms and suites of varying sizes, with deluxe doubles the ones to aim for.

Brown's Hotel (with entrances on both Dover Street and Albemarle Street—each leading from Piccadilly; phone 493-6020) has been a London fixture since the year Victoria acceded to the throne. That, if you have momentarily

forgotten, was 1837. Brown's carpeted floors are evocatively creaky. There's a paneled lounge for drinks and
what is arguably the most enjoyable afternoon tea of any
London hotel, traditional-decor restaurant, and 135 bedrooms and suites. Brown's hall porters are celebrated, and
with good reason. Where does one find better, more efficient, or more kind? Trusthouse Forte.

Capital Hotel (22 Basil Street; phone 589-5171) has for
some years been appreciated for its intimate charm. (There
are just 60 rooms and suites, and it's located on a convenient Knightsbridge street.) But its plain contemporary
decor did not, alas, win it any beauty contests. That is all
changing, with skilled interior designer Nina Campbell
(whose first hotel was Hambleton Hall in the Midlands)
transforming the interior, with typically exuberant treat-
ment blending traditional textiles and furniture with witty
Campbell innovations. You'll see what I mean in the guest
rooms she's had a hand in, at the bar-lounge, and in the
long-esteemed French restaurant, about which I comment
in a subsequent chapter.

Churchill Hotel (Portman Square; phone 486-5800):
Rooms and suites are Regency-style, and so are public
spaces, including what has to be the most beautiful hotel
coffee shop in London, not to mention the restaurant
called, appropriately enough, No. 10. (There is a sculpted
head of Sir Winston in the lobby.) Sunken tea lounge.

Claridge's Hotel (Brook Street; phone 629-8860), in the
heart of the smartest part of Mayfair, has made a specialty
of royalty over the years (since 1838, to be precise). The
original Claridges were a butler and his wife, a housekeep-
er who had worked for the gentry. But France's Empress
Eugénie signed the register in 1860, to be visited by no less
grand a lady than Queen Victoria. And the crowned heads

have not stopped since. Part of the staff still is liveried—a nice Claridge's touch this—and one drinks (tea or stronger stuff) in the handsome and high-ceilinged lobby-lounge rather than in a detached bar, the better to watch the clientele pass in review. Accommodations are elaborate, the proportion of suites is high, and the capacious Art Deco-era bathrooms—with original tilework and showers with immense octagonal heads—are a joy. Two restaurants, one of which is later evaluated. Member, Leading Hotels of the World.

Connaught Hotel (Carlos Place; phone 499-7070) is quite as though some English friends were putting you up at their turn-of-century townhouse. Accommodations—of which there are not all that many (the total of rooms and suites is 106)—are quietly deluxe. You would not be terribly surprised to meet His Majesty, Edward VII, in the paneled bar, which is, in and of itself, a worthy destination for the thirsty. And the restaurant warrants additional comment on a later page. Note that the Connaught accepts only MasterCard—no other plastic. Member, Leading Hotels of the World, Relais et Châteaux.

Dorchester Hotel (Park Lane; phone 629-8888) is, or at least always has been for me, an extraordinary hotel experience. The luxury is the kind that English interior designers—Oliver Messel, for one—create so well, combining traditional furnishings with contemporary fabrics and colors, with the results warm and welcoming. This is an exceptional place to eat, too: tea in the recently enlarged Promenade Lounge, casual lunches in the strikingly good-looking Cocktail Bar, and exceptional meals in the svelte, French-accented Terrace Restaurant and the English-fare Grill Room [see London To Eat (and Drink)]. Ordinary bedrooms are particularly spacious. But suites—the many regular ones and the super-luxurious Roof Garden series

—can be sumptuous. Ask for front accommodations, and your view is of Hyde Park. A Regent International hotel.

Dukes Hotel (35 St. James's Place; phone 491-4840) is one you either look for or are taken to, but I'll wager it's not one you'll casually pass by. And therein lies its charm. St. James's Place is a cul-de-sac off St. James's Street, closer to Pall Mall than to Piccadilly. Of the 50-plus rooms, those on lower floors tend to be compact, those higher up (recently created) are good-size and smartly traditional in look. There are, in addition, 14 super suites with big baths and, as a bonus, kitchens; and a paneled bar and a restaurant about which I write more on a later page, and a delightfully hospitable staff. Member, Prestige Hotels.

Grosvenor House Hotel (90 Park Lane; phone 449-6363) went up in the late twenties. Its architect, Sir Edwin Lutyens, was the very same whom the Crown had earlier commissioned to design a new capital for India when it was determined that it was time to move on from Calcutta to New Delhi. Lobby is big and humming. Residential wings—they are connected by a central pavilion housing the lobby and the public rooms—boast zingy accommodations. (The suites are sumptuous.) There are fine restaurants (that termed Ninety Park Lane is exceptional) and drinking parlors, and tea in the lounge remains a happy London pastime. A Trusthouse Forte Exclusive Division hotel.

Howard Hotel (Temple Place; phone 836-3555)— Thames-front and with venerable Somerset House (a government building) its next-door neighbor—is contemporary of facade but quite the reverse indoors, with an almost forbiddingly formal lobby-lounge based on traditional motifs, restaurant, bar, and 134 rooms and suites with marble baths; river-view ones are, of course, preferred.

Hyatt Carlton Tower Hotel (2 Cadogan Place; phone 235-5411): Credit Hyatt International for zeroing in on a class act of a London hotel—architecturally contemporary, albeit graceful, and situated in posh Belgravia, with shops and restaurants of both Knightsbridge and the King's Road equally close by—for its European flagship. When Hyatt took over, half a decade back, it embarked on an ongoing multimillion-pound refurbishment with style and flair. Much of the capacious lobby has become the Chinoiserie, traditionally furnished, but with Oriental accents, and serving as a café-lounge open early breakfast through casual lunch, afternoon tea, cocktails, and on into the late hours. One of the two restaurants, the Chelsea Room, was upgraded, while the other—specializing in beef—remain traditional in look. And guest rooms—228, all told—have been deftly restyled, with Spa Suites, each with whirlpool baths, especially handsome. Hyatt with a British accent? You bet. And it works.

Hyde Park Hotel (Knightsbridge; phone 235-2000) is surely—along with nearby Harrods department store—the most easily identifiable building in the Knightsbridge quarter, a perfectly splendid red-brick Victorian pile, towered and turreted and, alone among London hotels, with back rooms facing onto Hyde Park. You want to aim for one of those, to be awakened each morning by the clomp-clomp of the Horse Guards en route from barracks to the Admiralty. There are 180 soft-toned rooms and a score of spacious suites, high-ceilinged public areas that include a pair of restaurants (one of which is detailed in the next chapter), and a congenial lounge, as agreeable for afternoon tea as for cocktails. A Trusthouse Forte Exclusive Division hotel that is also a member of Leading Hotels of the World.

Inn on the Park (Hamilton Place/Park Lane; phone 499-

0888) successfully melds a contemporary facade and predominantly contemporary look with just enough of the
traditional to be distinctive. Really generous-size rooms
and suites; always humming, high-ceilinged lobby embracing a handsome lounge that's pleasant for tea and
drinks, pair of restaurants—both the Four Seasons and
Lanes—all have style. Suites, not surprisingly, are super,
but even standard rooms are exceptionally capacious; their
excellent baths are equipped with Floris soap (see London
To Buy). Service is nowhere more cordial or professional;
this is one of London's best-operated houses. A Four Seasons Hotel that is a member of the Prestige Hotels group
and of Leading Hotels of the World.

Inter-Continental London Hotel (Hamilton Place/Park
Lane; phone 409-3131) has a lot going for it. Location is
first—at Hyde Park Corner, looking over the park and just
opposite Apsley House, built as a townhouse for the first
Duke of Wellington and now an art-filled museum. Skilled
management is second. And facilities—500 traditional-
style rooms and suites with superbly equipped baths—is
third. There are a pair of restaurants (one, Le Soufflé, is
later counseled; the other is a late-hours coffee shop), a
pair of bars—one on the roof turns disco after dark—and a
chauffeur-equipped Rolls-Royce that will take you to or
from the airport or, for that matter, on town and country
tours. Along with the Inter-Continental Maui, in Hawaii,
and the Inter-Continental New York, this is my favorite in
the chain.

Londonderry Hotel (Park Lane; phone 493-7292): You
may—or may not—remember the original Londonderry
as unexceptionally contemporary, set between the London
Hilton and the Inn on the Park. Well, the mid-1980s saw a
long-term closing and a stem-to-stern refurbishing. Today's Londonderry has as its decor theme what might be

called Renaissance Revival, and very classy it is, with quite-grand public spaces, a restaurant with an extraordinarily beautiful painted ceiling, an amusing red plush bar, and 150 suites and rooms, with twin-bedded accommodations appreciably larger than rooms with double beds.

London Hilton on Park Lane (22 Park Lane; phone 493-8000) raised eyebrows among locals when it opened in the sixties. Muttering, muttering about those upstart colonials coming over to run a hotel—and a skyscraper of a hotel at that. Well, Hilton International pioneered in London, as in other parts of the world. After two fabulously successful decades, the hotel emerged into the late eighties with a new name—it had been called Hilton International London—and a new decor, as a consequence of a $7 million renovation. The clean-lined lobby took on a soft Georgian look with Chippendale and Hepplewhite furnishings; it opens onto a spacious lounge that welcomes guests for breakfast, casual lunches, afternoon tea, and cocktails. A marble staircase leads to the high-ceilinged and handsome British Harvest Restaurant. And the 24th through 27th floors—with nearly 20 new suites and close to 40 upgraded rooms—embrace the Vista Executive section of the hotel, with separate check-in and complimentary breakfast, snacks, and beverages for its premium-category guests.

London Marriott Hotel (Duke Street at Grosvenor Square; phone 493-1232) is the onetime Europa Hotel, attractively mock-Georgian with respect to facade, splendidly situated, and with but one drawback when Marriott took over: smallish rooms. Marriott management, to alleviate this problem, undertook elaborate renovations, eliminating many rooms in the process, to create larger guest quarters; there are now 17 snazzy suites and 212 rooms, with the Executive Doubles especially good-sized. The wood-paneled Diplomat Restaurant is French-inspired, there's a lively cocktail lounge, and the look throughout is handsomely traditional.

May Fair Hotel (Stratton Street, off Piccadilly; phone 629-7777): I first came to know the May Fair—its title quite correctly connotes grandness, for it was opened by King George V in the Roaring Twenties—in the course of attending a play in the legitimate theater sharing its name and building. Then, a few seasons back, Inter-Continental Hotels took over and spent £14 million to refurbish the 327 rooms and suites and replace their baths. Inter-Continental's design whiz, Neal Prince, was dispatched from headquarters in New York and beautifully redecorated the hotel in lush traditional style, transforming every room and creating a trio of super-suites that are among London's most opulent. There are a pair of restaurants—Le Château (worthy of later evaluation) and the casual Coffee Shop—and a pair of bars, not to mention a staff than which there is no kindlier or more efficient in London.

New Piccadilly Hotel (Piccadilly; phone 734-8000) dates back, in its original form, to 1908, when it was the talk of London. Its facade, arcaded at street level and topped by a dazzling colonnade of eight Corinthian pillars, is like no other in town. Recent decades saw the Piccadilly slide downhill. The principal restaurant, oak-paneled in the manner of the great hall of a country house, had become, on my last visit, a help-yourself-to-roast-beef carvery. Enter Gleneagles Hotels as new owner, which spent £16 million to create the New Piccadilly. There are just under 300 traditional-style rooms and suites. But this hotel puts its best foot forward in public spaces: Terrace Garden Restaurant (evaluated later) set behind columns of the facade; absolutely fabulous Gleneagles Club with really big swimming pool, gym, sauna, squash court, and café; boîte-disco, logically called the Music Room; kicky cocktail bar; sumptuous lounge that's a pleasure for afternoon tea; and, for nostalgia buffs of the old Piccadilly like me, the Oak Room—with original paneling of the old main dining room not only retained but restored and an Anglo-French menu about which I comment on a later page.

Ritz Hotel (Piccadilly; phone 493-8181), created by the legendary Caesar Ritz and for long both a London land-mark *and* a London institution, has been refurbished at considerable cost. The glass-roofed Palm Court—all pan-eled walls and crystal chandeliers and plasterwork picked out in gold—has become so popular for tea that you must book in advance. All the public spaces, especially the Louis XV-inspired restaurant (worthy of later evaluation), are beautiful, as is the old ballroom, now seeing service as the separately entered Ritz Casino. By all means, pop into the Ritz for a drink, tea, or a meal. Settling in is another matter, or at least has been, in my experience. I have found hall porters surly and/or inept and reception staff patro-nizing. Single rooms can be tiny. Corridor walls are hung with garish, posterlike paintings. And in an expensively refurbished, *really* costly, super-deluxe London hotel with but 144 suites and rooms, is there any excuse for bath-rooms without showers (I drew one, on one visit) or for bathrooms with their showers' hot-water taps inoperable (my luck, on another visit)? Member, Prestige Hotels.

St. James's Club (Park Place, off St. James's Street; phone 629-7688) occupies a capacious Victorian townhouse that has been smartly fashioned into a private club that oper-ates as a hotel—with nearly 30 smashing Art Deco suites and 16 similarly smart doubles, the lot with superb baths. There are lounges on the street floor and a cocktail bar and excellent French-accented restaurant in the basement, to which members may bring guests. "Club" in the title means just that. You must be a member—there are annual dues and elected officers and board—to stay at St. James's. *However,* overseas visitors need not be members for an initial stay, so long as they've booked in advance.

Savoy Hotel (Strand; phone 836-4343) is the epitome of Victorian London, dating to 1889 and in the hurly-burly quarter adjacent to the City that is chock-full of fine specimens of Victorian architecture. You're away from Mayfair and the West End here, but the Savoy is convenient for theater and opera buffs and those with business in the City. There are 200 no-two-alike, quietly traditional rooms, of which half a hundred are suites (those facing the Thames are the loveliest); two dining rooms (the Savoy Grill warrants comment on a later page; the River Restaurant features dancing at dinner); convivial bar that serves the best dry martinis in town; Thames Foyer for tea and pretheater snacks; and extraordinary private-party rooms, including eight named for Gilbert & Sullivan operas— appropriate, given the Savoy's founder: Savoyard impresario Richard d'Oyly Carte. In my experience, one of Europe's best-operated hotels; it's always a pleasure. Member, Leading Hotels of the World.

Sheraton Park Tower Hotel (101 Knightsbridge; phone 235-8050), occupying a circular 18-story structure, has become a Knightsbridge landmark, with Hyde Park views from many of its period-decor, marble-bathed suites and rooms, a later-recommended restaurant, a bar-lounge, and a convenient location; with major stores like Harvey Nichols and Harrods near-neighbors. Very smart, indeed.

Westbury Hotel (New Bond Street; phone 629-7755) has two major pluses: an inspired location, as convenient for shops as for theater, and professional service. There is a good restaurant, much frequented by Londoners, and the popular Polo Bar. Rooms, however, can run small, although efforts have been made to redesign them so as to afford more space. Trusthouse Forte.

SELECTED FIRST-CLASS HOTELS

Basil Street Hotel (Basil Street; phone 581-3311) is so attractively decorated with antiques and so agreeably located in Knightsbridge that it is never wanting for clients. Book way in advance for this one. The lounges could be those of a great house in town or even in the country. There is a reasonably priced coffee shop. But, alas, the main restaurant is not what it once was; a recently sampled breakfast was sadly disagreeable. And note: Only about half of the 123 rooms have baths.

Belgravia Sheraton Hotel (20 Chesham Place; phone 235-6040): Sensing the need for an intimate hotel in the fashionable Belgrave Square quarter, Sheraton Hotels bought the London Belgravia and closed it down, the while spending £4 million on a stem-to-stern refurbishing. The result was the Belgravia Sheraton, a 90-room house that caught on immediately with business, as well as pleasure, visitors. Take your choice of one-bedroom or studio suites or king- or queen-size doubles; all have spanking new phone-equipped baths, with the decor theme a kind of modified traditional, which carries into public spaces. These include a well-operated restaurant (whose prix-fixe lunches and dinners are sound buys and include wine and coffee) and lobby-bar-lounge in which is served morning coffee, a bargain-tabbed buffet lunch, and afternoon tea.

Berners Hotel (10 Berners Street; phone 636-1629) is an oldie, happily retaining period decor in public spaces but with its 240 rooms all updated. Restaurant, bar, and a location convenient to Oxford Street.

Cadogan Thistle Hotel (95 Sloane Street; phone 235-7141) is an older house of moderate size, Edwardian-handsome, with super bedrooms and suites (Oscar Wilde was arrested in one of the latter, the management advises); a bar named for Lily Langtry, a onetime resident; a reliable restaurant; and a lounge made to order for well-priced afternoon tea or a drink. Lovely.

Cavendish Hotel (Jermyn Street; phone 930-2111), just opposite Fortnum & Mason, is a modern version of a well-known oldie that occupied the same space. Location is convenient. Rooms are functional, but public areas—including a restaurant and a cozy bar—are more inviting. Trusthouse Forte.

Chesterfield Hotel (35 Charles Street; phone 491-2622) does not take its name lightly. An eighteenth-century Earl of Chesterfield was its builder and original occupant. There are today just over 80 rooms, all consistently well equipped, and delightful public spaces, the range, a library-like lounge through a bar giving onto the garden. With an elegant—and excellent—restaurant.

Cumberland Hotel (Marble Arch; phone 262-1234) is British hotelkeeping at its middle-level best. The idea is solid comfort rather than luxury. There are more than 900 rooms, and all are cheery and well equipped; several restaurants (one of which is later evaluated) and bars, as well. Trusthouse Forte.

11 Cadogan Gardens Hotel (11 Cadogan Gardens; phone 937-8170) occupies a quartet of contiguous Edwardian-era houses on a fashionable Chelsea street just off Sloane Square. All 50 of the rooms—no two of which are alike either in size or decor—have baths, and of these not quite half are shower equipped. Main-floor lounge is antiques furnished, and a treat is inclusion of a whopping big English breakfast—served in rooms—in the daily rate.

Flemings Hotel (10 Half Moon Street, off Piccadilly; phone 499-2964) is a onetime budget-category house favored for its good location that has been thoroughly refurbished in traditional style—and upgraded in rank. You no longer go for the low tabs, but rather for the attractive accommodations—there are 135 rooms with good baths, bar-lounge, and convenient restaurant.

Goring Hotel (15 Beeston Place, off Grosvenor Gardens, near Buckingham Palace; phone 834-8211) is a honey of a family-run (third generation) house in gracious traditional style, with capacious public areas, convenient restaurant with English favorites always on its menu, a hundred no-two-quite-alike rooms (ask for one overlooking the hotel's big garden), and a delightful staff, many of whose members are long on scene.

Grosvenor Hotel (101 Buckingham Palace Road, adjacent to Victoria Station; phone 834-9494) is the very model of a mid-category Victorian palace: high-ceilinged public areas, with a grand staircase dead center, open-late restaurant, spacious bar-lounge, and showers in some of the 356 well-equipped rooms' baths. Location—near Buckingham Palace—is such that when the Guard changes, it marches past the Grosvenor. Specify the main building over the annex-wing. Excellent value.

Holiday Inn Chelsea (Sloane Street; phone 235-4377) looks nothing like your standard Holiday Inn because it was not built as one: tasteful, traditionally influenced decor, a couple of hundred well-equipped rooms, pleasant cocktail lounge, restaurant encircling the indoor swimming pool.

Holiday Inn Marble Arch (George Street; phone 723-1277) is a few short blocks north of the landmark that designates it. It has 245 comfortable rooms, round-the-clock room service, restaurant, coffee shop, and bar, as well as convenient ice-cube machines on every floor.

Holiday Inn Mayfair (Berkeley Street, off Piccadilly; phone 493-8282): My goodness, time flies. When I first knew this location, it housed the old Berkeley Hotel, before it built new quarters in Knightsbridge (above). Next, I found myself inspecting a rebuilt hostelry on the site, called the Bristol. On a recent stroll along Berkeley Street, I discovered that the Bristol had become the Holiday Inn Mayfair—a meld of modern and Louis XV, embracing not quite 190 rooms and suites with well-equipped baths, reliable restaurant, bar-lounge, and friendly staff.

Kensington Close Hotel (Wright's Lane; phone 937-8170): All 350 rooms' baths have showers and there are fine views from the upper floors, not to mention such amenities as a swimming pool, sauna, and terrace.

Kensington Palace Thistle Hotel (corner of De Vere Gardens and Kensington Road; phone 937-8121) is an agreeably modernized house of some age, just opposite Kensington Gardens and midway between Kensington High Street shops and the Victoria and Albert and neighboring museums. There are a pair of restaurants and a pair of bars, as well as 316 rooms; singles, as well as doubles, vary in size.

Lowndes Thistle Hotel (21 Lowndes Street; phone 235-6020) has a stark, contemporary facade that does not prepare one for the interiors, which are late twentieth-century emulations of the Georgian genius of Robert Adam. Lobby, Adam Room Restaurant, and even bedrooms are Adam style, while the bar is exuberant Chinese Chippendale. Smart.

Mountbatten Hotel (Seven Dials at Monmouth Street; phone 836-4000)—for long the Shaftesbury Hotel, in the Covent Garden area, convenient to theaters—emerged after extensive mid-1980s refurbishing with a new name, new management, 127 rooms (singles are small), and public spaces—Burma Room Restaurant, Broadlands Lounge, for example—called after significant places and events in the life of the late Lord Mountbatten of Burma, a member of the Royal Family who was a World War II hero and the last viceroy of India. The aforementioned Broadlands Lounge (its name derives from that of the Mountbattens' house in Hampshire, about which I write in *Britain at Its Best*) brims with interesting Mountbatten mementos, but one has the distinct feeling that Lord Louis might not be pleased with the poor reproductions of a portrait of him, dotted about, especially in the suite that takes his name.

New Mandeville Hotel (Mandeville Place; phone 435-5599) is an exceptionally tasteful, middle-category house but a stroll from Oxford and Regent streets. Rooms could be larger, but there is no denying their good looks and good baths—all shower-equipped. Four places to eat: formal restaurant, cheery coffee shop, traditional-style pub, and tearoom.

Pastoria Hotel (St. Martin's Street; phone 930-8641) has the advantages of a convenient Leicester Square situation, and an overwhelming majority of its 50-odd rooms have a bath. Restaurant-bar.

Portman Inter-Continental Hotel (22 Portman Square; phone 486-5844) went up in the early 1970s, when "contemporary" could be equated with "stark," with respect to interiors. Well, Inter-Continental management changed all that, with a mid-1980s refurbishing which saw the big lobby emerge warmly paneled and chandeliered; the highly respected, French-accented restaurant was renamed Truffles and redecorated (it is evaluated on a later page, along with the hotel's pair of popular-price eateries); the Silver Room emerged as a smart cocktail lounge; and traditional furnishings gradually transformed the 278 rooms and suites. Friendly.

Royal Garden Hotel (Kensington High Street; phone 937-8000) is a big mid-sixties palace, with an immense high-ceilinged lobby, quartet of restaurants (one later evaluated), equally generous choice of bars, 500 rooms and suites, and situation at the edge of Kensington Gardens, with views of Kensington Palace. Very pleasant. A Rank hotel.

Royal Horseguards Thistle Hotel (Whitehall Court; phone 839-3400) has going for it a location overlooking the Thames near Parliament. Without, the Royal Horseguards is Victorian. Within is a contemporary hotel: sleek-lined lobby; compact red, black, and white guest rooms; and an ice machine on every floor. Bar and coffee shop.

Royal Lancaster Hotel (Lancaster Terrace, north of Hyde Park; phone 262-6737) is among the choicest of the skyscrapers, with a traditional decor, 467 nice-looking bedrooms and suites, and a pair each of restaurants and bars. A Rank hotel.

Royal Westminster Thistle Hotel (Buckingham Palace Road; phone 834-1821) might well be called the Royal Buckingham. It is a near neighbor of the palace, to the point where the Royal Guard passes by en route to Changing ceremonies at the palace's front gate. Behind the clean-lined facade are attractive public spaces, including an inviting bar and restaurant, functional guest rooms, and ice machines on every floor.

Russell Hotel (Russell Square; phone 837-6470) is the Grande Dame of Bloomsbury—a magnificent Edwardian pile, with one of the great facades of London, a marble-arched and pillared lobby, and similarly impressive public rooms, including a restaurant, grill room, pair of bars, and a lounge where afternoon tea—particularly welcome after a visit to the nearby British Museum   is served. Bedrooms have been modernized; some baths have showers. Trusthouse Forte.

Selfridge Thistle Hotel (Orchard Street; phone 408-2080) is most definitely to be associated with Selfridges department store on Oxford Street. It is right next door, with 304 rooms, handsome restaurant, coffee shop, bar, and—hear this, shoppers—separate entrance of its very own to the vast, tempting department store adjoining. Very attractive.

Stafford Hotel (St. James's Place, just off St. James's Street; phone 493-0111) is but a hop and a skip from Dukes (see above) and is quite as old-school and as charming, with a loyal army of repeat customers, again like Dukes. There are 70 rooms—some more attractive and more recently redecorated than others. The inviting little bar has a Louis XV look. It and the adjoining restaurant (worthy of later evaluation) have their own (optional) entrances on Blue Ball Yard. Member, Prestige Hotels.

Tower Thistle Hotel (St. Katharine's Way; phone 481-2575) is perhaps the most romantically located hotel in London—just across the street from Her Majesty's Tower of London. The hotel is up-to-the-minute modern, with more than 800 rooms and a slew of bars and restaurants. But mind, you are *way* east, a couple of blocks from Tower Hill tube station—your quickest link with the West End.

Waldorf Hotel (Aldwych; phone 836-2400) is a landmark on the arc-shaped thoroughfare that leads off the Strand and backs on to what has become Fleet Street. Its glory is a high-ceilinged lounge (a major destination for tea). The restaurant, all crystal chandeliers and Ionic columns, is smart. There are 310 bedrooms and suites, which Trusthouse Forte management has modernized.

SELECTED MODERATE HOTELS

Alexander Hotel (9 Sumner Place; phone 581-1591): Though with interiors by no means as stylish as those of its across-the-street neighbor, Number Sixteen Sumner Place (below), the Alexander is agreeable; a clutch of refurbished elderly houses, in which all doubles have baths and some singles have showers. Restaurant, lounge.

Bedford Hotel (83 Southampton Row; phone 636-7822) is a favorite with visitors for whom the British Museum or University of London are prime destinations. There is a garden, with restaurant and bar overlooking it, and some of the 180-plus rooms' baths have showers.

Bloomsbury Crest Hotel (Coram Street; phone 837-1200) is just north and east of Russell Square, in the British Museum-University of London area. It may lack atmosphere, but it is big (all 247 rooms' baths have showers); restaurant, coffee shop, bar.

Charing Cross Hotel (Strand; phone 839-7282), attached to Charing Cross Railway Station, is a turn-of-century souvenir of an era when hotels were built with high ceilings, elaborate plasterwork, and palatial reception areas. Today's visitors enjoy the style of the old with contemporary facilities like private baths and convenient wine-dine facilities, especially the Betjeman Carving Restaurant—an all-you-like, beef-lamb-pork eatery.

Clifton Ford Hotel (Welbeck Street; phone 486-6600) is conveniently located on Welbeck Street, a bit north of Oxford Street; restaurant, bar.

Ebury Court Hotel (26 Ebury Street; phone 730-8147) embraces a quartet of elderly joined houses. Corridors are irregular because of the way the houses are joined; not all the rooms have baths. The restaurant is exceptional. Victoria Station is close by, and both the Piccadilly and Knightsbridge areas are short bus rides away. Charming.

Embassy House Hotel (31 Queen's Gate; phone 884-7222) is nicely situated near Kensington High Street. Elderly from without, it surprises within: All 70 rooms have showers in their baths. Coffee shop, bar.

Hyde Park Towers Hotel (Inverness Terrace; phone 229-9461) is just off Bayswater Road, north of Hyde Park. It's an updated building, with cheery rooms (all of whose baths have showers), coffee shop, and bar.

Ivanhoe Hotel (Bloomsbury Street; phone 636-5601) is no-frills, behind a rather forbidding facade in the British Museum area. Rooms are pleasant enough, housekeeping is good, and there are a moderate-priced restaurant, café, and bar.

Kenilworth Hotel (97 Great Russell Street; phone 637-3477) is, not unsurprisingly—given its name—an across-the-street neighbor of the above-described Ivanhoe in Bloomsbury. It, too, has a restaurant and bar and has had a thorough—relatively recent and attractive—facelift.

Kensington Court Hotel (33 Nevern Place at Templeton Place; phone 370-5191) is near the Earl's Court exhibition center and the tube station of that name. It's out of the way, but the baths of all its modern rooms are shower equipped; restaurant and bar.

Kingsley Hotel (Bloomsbury Way; phone 242-5881) is a quiet British Museum neighbor. It's a good value, with well over half its 175 rooms equipped with baths, if not showers. The restaurant is of the help-yourself-to-roast-beef variety, and there's a bar.

L'Hôtel (Basil Street; phone 589-6286) is not only a neighbor of the Capital Hotel (above) but shares the same owners, if not the same smart ambience. This relatively new establishment has but eleven rooms and a one-bedroom suite. Decor motif is college-dorm maple—nothing fancy, mind you—and each room has its own bath, with hand-showers attached to tubs. There's a wine bar-restaurant in the basement, French style and popular with neighborhood regulars.

London Elizabeth Hotel (Lancaster Terrace at Bayswater

Road; phone 402-6641) is just opposite the Royal Lancaster Hotel. Rooms are satisfactory, but the big plus is a French-operated restaurant.

Londoner Hotel (Welbeck Street; phone 935-4442) is a same-street neighbor of the Clifton Ford. There are 120 rooms, a restaurant, and a bar, and the location, a bit north of Oxford Street, is convenient.

Milestone Hotel (1 Kensington Court; phone 937-0991) is late nineties, with vistas of Kensington Gardens, and 50 of its 80-odd rooms have baths; restaurant, bar.

Mostyn Hotel (Portman Street; phone 935-2361) is a Portman Square-area hostelry, with Oxford Street nearby. It's elderly, but with updated bedrooms, all of which now have baths; pretty restaurant, pair of bars.

Mount Royal Hotel (Bryanston Street; phone 629-8040) is a neighbor of the earlier described Cumberland, though smaller—it has but 700 rooms to the Cumberland's 900. Emphasis is on comfort at a good price. Restaurant and bar.

Number Sixteen Sumner Place Hotel (16 Sumner Place; phone 589-5232) occupies a joined trio of elderly, attractively decorated, well-maintained Kensington houses. Breakfast only.

Rembrandt Hotel (Thurloe Place; phone 589-8100) is convenient to Harrods. It's Edwardian in origin, with a carvery-style roast-beef restaurant and bar-lounge.

Royal Court Hotel (Sloane Square; phone 730-9191) is at once conveniently situated and well equipped (restaurant, two bars), with those of its recently refurbished rooms the ones to specify.

Rubens Hotel (Buckingham Palace Road; phone 834-6600), with its opposite-the-palace location, has 150 updated rooms. Restaurant and bar, appropriately enough, considering the location, are embellished with likenesses of former residents of the big house across the street.

St. Ermin's Hotel (Caxton Street; phone 222-7888) has 252 well-fitted rooms; high-ceilinged, still-Victorian main lounge; grill room; and bar.

Sherlock Holmes Hotel (Baker Street; phone 486-6161) is included here for two reasons. First is because it is a comfortable, medium-size (149 rooms) modern hotel in a reasonably convenient part of town, north of Oxford Street. Second is because it alone on Baker Street pays tribute to the fictional detective with whose name the street is synonymous. Volumes of Holmes are on sale, and there are public rooms named for the good Watson and the evil Moriarty.

Strand Palace Hotel (Strand; phone 836-8080) is value-packed. Its exterior is elderly, but its functional, 800-room interior is reasonably up-to-date; there are varied eat-drink locales, including an all-you-can-eat, roast beef restaurant. Trusthouse Forte.

Stratford Court Hotel (350 Oxford Street; phone 629-7474) is near department stores and Bond Street boutiques; has had a thorough and relatively recent refurbishing; and offers pleasant rooms, carvery-type restaurant, and bar.

Wilbraham Hotel (1 Wilbraham Place; phone 730-8296)

is a perfect charmer of a Victorian house, all dark paneling and antiques, with a spic-and-span look to both public rooms (these include a good restaurant, the Beurre Fondu, evaluated in the next chapter) and guest rooms, of which there are no two alike. Location, near Sloane Square, is super.

Willett Hotel (32 Sloane Gardens; phone 730-0634) is small (17 rooms) and simple but clean, with a full English breakfast part of the tab.

STAYING AT THE AIRPORTS

Gatwick Hilton International Hotel (phone (0293) 518-080) is a part of the Gatwick Airport complex, with access to its terminal through a covered passageway from its striking atrium-lobby. The 380 rooms and suites are soundproofed and tasteful, with welcome American-style plumbing in the baths, restaurant, traditional-style pub, lobby bar, indoor pool and health club, and a slew of conference rooms for business meetings and meals. *Luxury.*

Sheraton Heathrow Hotel (phone 759-2424) is a five-minute drive (via hotel shuttle bus) from the airport. This is a biggie: 440 really comfortable rooms, restaurant-grill, late-hours coffee shop, bar-lounge, indoor pool, sauna. Very comfortable. *Luxury.*

5

London To Eat (and Drink)

SETTING THE RESTAURANT SCENE

First, let me point out that I have dined, lunched, and often breakfasted in the restaurants carefully selected for evaluation in these pages; they are divided into three price groups: *Luxury, First Class,* and *Moderate.* Next, let me urge that you forget much of what you've heard about British food. With respect to restaurants, London is an all-planet leader, with some serving British food at its best and with others serving the great foreign cuisines. You will no more have a problem dining well in London than you would in New York or Geneva or Rome or Toronto.

As a general guide, British fare is delicious when it's simple—roasts of beef, lamb, and pork; beef steaks and grilled lamb chops (one of Britain's best food buys, incidentally); game (of which the British eat a lot); fresh salmon, trout, and other fish; savory pies—beef and kidney, chicken; accompanying vegetables when they're fresh and—not always the case—not overcooked; breakfasts; baked goods (cakes [called *gâteaux*, the French term, when they're fancy], pies, cookies [called biscuits], and, increasingly rarely, breads); and the makings of afternoon tea (*please* don't call it "high"—that's a synonym for an inelegant evening meal)—finger sandwiches, the aforementioned sweet stuff, and, if it's a cream tea, a caloric blob of thick, Devonshire-type cream served with jam and the biscuits called scones.

Cheeses—Cheddar and Stilton, but also lesser-known species like Wensleydale, Caerphilly, Derby, Double Gloucester, and Lancashire—are invariably offered as an alternative to dessert, and, also invariably, they are excellent. As a general rule, it's worth asking that sauces and gravies be served on the side; except in top-rung, British-cuisine restaurants (or authentic French and Italian spots), they can be gloopy and floury.

Food-serving pubs (I recommend many on the pages following) make for the most economical, swiftest, and—very often—very tasty lunches. Last but not least, be grateful for restaurants operated by Italians, Frenchmen, Chinese, Danes, Indians, Spaniards, and Greeks, who, in recent decades, have added a welcome international dimension to the British cuisine scene.

THE BRITISH BREAKFAST

Breakfast, traditionally—along with afternoon tea—the best meal of the British day, is no longer always of the quality it used to be, at least in hotels. At its best—fresh-squeezed orange juice, porridge or cold cereal with cream, eggs prepared to your order (scrambled, fried, boiled, poached), crispy bacon (English bacon, unless well done, is not necessarily to North Americans' liking), well-cooked sausages and/or kippered herring, coffee with some character—there is no better breakfast in the world.

But hotels occasionally take to scrambling eggs in enormous batches, and in advance; they do likewise even with fried eggs. Soft-boiled eggs upon occasion may arrive

hard, jam may come in difficult-to-open plastic packets—
that kind of thing. (Toast now, as always, is served cold, in
metal racks especially designed for the purpose. But that is
a British eccentricity that longtime Anglophiles like me
have long since come to accept.)

It is worth my mentioning, at this point, that London's
luxury-category hotels invariably do *not* include breakfast
in rates, while *other* hotels may or may not. Even when
breakfast is included, inquire as to whether it is a full
(a.k.a. English) breakfast or a simple fruit juice, rolls or
toast, and coffee Continental breakfast. Still another
breakfast point: Many hotels thoughtfully include coffee/
tea-making equipment in rooms, with packets of instant
coffee and tea bags and sometimes even a chocolate-wafer
bar, as well. (The Trusthouse Forte chain deserves com-
mendation for pioneering in this respect, in all but its
poshest hotels.) Add a piece of fruit that you've purchased
while traveling, and you've the making of your own Continental breakfast.

SELECTED ENGLISH-CONTINENTAL
RESTAURANTS

Bates (11 Henrietta Street; phone 240-7600) belies its
plain decor with corking good food—some of the best in
the Covent Garden quarter. The three-course table d'hôte
is temptingly tabbed and tasty—running to cream of
mushroom soup or ravioli to begin; followed by grilled
salmon, supreme of duck or *grenadin* of veal; and conclud-
ing with a superb *ganache* of Belgian chocolate buried
under bittersweet chocolate sauce flecked with almonds.
Lovely service. *First Class.*

Beurre Fondu (Wilbraham Hotel, 1 Wilbraham Place;
phone 730-8296): Continental and English dishes served

in a Victorian atmosphere of white napery, dark-wood paneling, fresh flowers. Roasts, grills, and desserts are very good, indeed. *Moderate.*

Buttery (Berkeley Hotel, Knightsbridge; phone 235-6000) is recommended for its remarkably well-priced buffet lunch—cold meats, hot dishes, salads, sweets, the lot delicious and the setting a handsome room in one of London's finest hotels. *Moderate.*

Café Royal (68 Regent Street; phone 437-9090) bespeaks Edwardian opulence. Menu blends the classic style of France—a duck *pâté*, for example, or *truite meunière aux pistaches*—with English specialties like bread pudding and roast lamb. The wine list is long and expert. There is a choice of rooms, with the Grill the smartest. *Luxury.*

Causerie (Claridge's Hotel, Brook Street; phone 629-8860) serves a celebrated luncheon buffet—an appetizing, Anglo-accented smorgasbord. And the Causerie is worth knowing about for post-theater dinners. *First Class.*

Connaught Hotel Restaurant (Carlos Place; phone 499-7070): If it is less exuberant than the Café Royal (above), this very proper dining room of a very proper hotel is no less Edwardian, with its look running to dark woods, starched white napery-cum-fresh flowers, gleaming silver, and impeccably tuxedoed waiters, every one of them, as far as I can perceive, skilled and smiling. Fare is overwhelmingly—and authentically—French, albeit with British overtones. By that, I mean you will be as happy with the extraordinary mix of *hors d'oeuvres au choix*, selected from a groaning two-tier trolley—*pâtés* and terrines, salamis and salads—as with the chicken pie that is an every-Sunday tradition. Roast beef and lamb chops are standbys, too; no less so are Gallic *quenelles de haddock* and *entrecôte grillée*. Waiters will happily let you choose mini-portions of two or three sweets from the wagon. French pastries are exemplary, but you ignore the Connaught's apple and black currant pie and its bread and butter pudding at your peril. The three-course prix-fixe lunch is one of the best buys in London. Precede it—or dinner—with a drink in the hotel's paneled bar. (And bear in mind that the Connaught, for some inexplicable reason, accepts but one credit card—MasterCard.) In my view, one of London's best restaurants. *Luxury*.

Dukes Hotel Restaurant (35 St. James's Place, off St. James's Street; phone 491 4840): Quarters tend to be cramped in this tastefully decorated restaurant—you overhear everyone else's conversations, and some are worth eavesdropping on. More to the point, however, the food is good Anglo-French, with creative touches. How about opening, for example, with a pair of eggshells filled with scrambled eggs, one flavored with lobster, the other with smoked salmon and truffles? Consider an entrée of filet of beef in a Madeira sauce topped with oysters or breast of duck served in tandem with a crispy duck salad. Have chocolate cake to conclude. *First Class*.

Ebury Court Hotel Restaurant (26 Ebury Street; phone 730-8147) is a London sleeper, traditional in look, if not always in menu. Dishes are as diverse as *poule basquaise* (chicken flamed in brandy, with red and green peppers, onions, and tomatoes), veal Cordon Bleu, minute steak, and a variety of tasty omelets. Home-baked bread as well. *First Class*.

Garden Café (Royal Garden Hotel, Kensington High Street; phone 937-8000): A well-priced, well-prepared three-course-and-coffee lunch or dinner—shrimp cocktail or soup, roast beef, dessert or cheese—in an attractive setting with views of Kensington Gardens (and Kensington Palace) as a bonus, is not to be despised. *Moderate.*

Grange (39 King Street; phone 240-2939) occupies a building of indeterminate vintage, on a difficult-to-locate City street. But the search is worthwhile. The Grange is a looker—subtle tones of brown, black, and white are used in the decor, from walls and ceiling to table linens and china. Good bets are *boeuf bourguignon,* a Middle-Eastern lamb kebab, or poached salmon. Roast duckling, with honey and orange, is delicious, too. *Luxury.*

General Trading Co. Café (144 Sloane Street, at Sloane Square; phone 730-6400) is a worth-knowing-about source of sustenance, breakfast through tea, not excluding morning—and, for that matter, all-day—coffee and made-on-premises cookies. Shepherd's pie is a good bet at midday, but there are French-inspired dishes, too. *Moderate.*

Hyde Park Hotel Grill Room (Knightsbridge; phone 235-2000), one of the two spiffy restaurants of a spiffy hotel, is a happy choice at midday, when it offers a generous buffet lunch—both hot and cold choices, with desserts included—and still another three-course table d'hôte, which might run to *pâté maison* or the day's soup, roast beef with Yorkshire pudding or grilled lamb chops, and dessert following. Pricier à la carte at dinner, but at lunch: *First Class.*

Lanes (Inn on the Park, Hamilton Place/Park Lane; phone 499-0888) is smartly contemporary and expertly staffed, with its ace-in-the-hole a fabulous cold buffet—salads, seafood, meats—from which you help yourself, as a first course, in connection with the prix-fixe lunch or dinner. Go midday and there's still another tempter: Wine is included. Grilled lamb chops constitute a winning entrée. *First Class.*

Le Château (May Fair Hotel, Stratton Street; phone 629-7777) is at once central—just off Piccadilly—and as convenient for lunch and dinner as for after-theater or Sunday brunch. It embraces a pair of intimate rooms, their walls surfaced in fabric, their ceilings handsomely tentlike, their tables set in pale pink linen with cut crystal adding sparkle, their waiters tailcoated. Fare is a successful hybrid—France, England, and the U.S. (where the landlord, Inter-Continental Hotels, is based)—with expertly prepared game (grouse, venison, partridge, pheasant) among specialties and the wine list extraordinary. The à la carte is expensive, but the table d'hôte, at both lunch and dinner, is sound value. Super service. *Luxury.*

Leith's (92 Kensington Park Road; phone 229-4481) occupies an elderly house with the decor no less original than the menu: game casseroles, for example, seafood bisques, a variety of made-on-the-premises *pâtés*, both meat and fish. *Luxury.*

Lyons Corner House (450 Strand, just off Trafalgar Square; phone 930-9381): First of the multilevel restaurant chain—long-beloved of foreign visitors (myself included) and Britons alike—to return after its 1970s demise, this Lyons has a main-floor coffee shop for breakfast, short orders, and tea; and a basement restaurant for more substantial meals, built around favorites like steak and kidney pie, and fish and chips. *Moderate.*

Masters (190 Queen's Gate; phone 581-5666)—worth knowing about in connection with visits to the nearby Kensington museums and Royal Albert Hall—combines traditional decor with a deliciously contemporary menu and a warm welcome from manager Nick Tarayan. The à la carte is fairly extensive, but I counsel the multichoice table d'hôte, which might open with cream of fennel and leek soup or a mushroom-tarragon terrine, continue with strips of beef in a juniper berry sauce or ballantine of chicken served with a hazelnut *mousse*, and conclude with a range of desserts or cheese; along with coffee and a plate of confected-on-premises sweetmeats. Service is delightful. *First Class.*

Oak Room (New Piccadilly Hotel, Piccadilly; phone 734-8000): The oak paneling of this splendidly proportioned room has, in the course of a brilliant refurbishing, been picked out in gold. Venetian crystal chandeliers hang from the ceiling, its stuccowork in hues of brown and tan. Go at dinner and a pianist plays Chopin from a white baby grand, while you indulge in a *nouvelle*-accented meal from an à la carte menu. Consider opening with a scallop-crayfish-lobster salad or seafood-stuffed ravioli. There are half a dozen fish entrées; sea bass topped with a chicken-salmon *mousse* is one such. And there are twice that many meat dishes, including filet of veal teamed with veal sweetbreads, Armagnac-sauced duckling, and lamb filet in a mushroom-truffle sauce. Desserts are no less inventive. And service is expert and attentive. *Luxury.*

Pub and Bakery (Portman Inter-Continental Hotel, 22 Portman Square; phone 486-5844): You've just come from a morning at the Wallace Collection or the bustle of Oxford Street shops and it's lunchtime. Portman Square is a pleasant stroll away, with the lures of these contiguous eateries off the Portman Hotel's lobby including onion soup, roast beef sandwiches, *quiche Lorraine,* and chicken-and-chive pie. *Moderate.*

Ritz Hotel Restaurant (Piccadilly; phone 493-8181) is one

of the most beautiful rooms in Europe, a generously proportioned Louis XV chamber giving onto the hotel's
walled garden, the severe black of the waiters' tails in
pleasing contrast to the pale walls, ceiling, and
plasterwork. Fare is Anglo-French and, in my experience,
deftly and smilingly served—and delicious. Good-value
set lunches. *Luxury.*

Sheraton Park Tower Hotel Restaurant (101 Knightsbridge; phone 235-8050): This circular tower of a hotel, a
Knightsbridge landmark, has replaced its two conventional restaurants—one a coffee shop, the other posher—with
a single eatery, dubbed The (with a capital "T") Restaurant,
that's open from early breakfast through late evening. A
glass-walled and domed conservatory—Art Deco in
style—it is worth knowing about after theater, when a
supper of, say, onion soup and a brace of perfectly boiled
lamb chops with a crisp salad fill the bill, accompanied by
one of the wines from an excellent French list. Splendid
service. Depending on when you go, *Moderate-First Class.*

Stafford Hotel Restaurant (St. James's Place; phone 493-
0111) is quiet of ambience, traditional in decor, and almost
completely French-staffed, with interesting French-
accented dishes (lobster bisque, *salade Niçoise*, calf's liver *à
l'orange*, sweetbreads Gloria), as well as English standbys
like potted shrimp and mixed grill. There are well-priced
prix-fixe menus at both lunch and dinner. *First Class.*

Terrace Garden (New Piccadilly Hotel, Piccadilly; phone
734-8000), strikingly glass roofed and affording super
views, is set behind the colonnaded facade of this handsome hotel, and is at once convenient for lunch—the
range is a club sandwich or a chef salad through sirloin
steak and grilled veal chops—and for after the play; theaters are close by. *First Class.*

Waltons (121 Walton Street, not far from the Victoria and Albert Museum in Kensington; phone 584-0000) is a looker; decor is an agreeable mix of gray, gold, and chrome; management is cordial; and fare, an Anglo-International meld, is delicious. Three-course set lunches—*rillettes* of salmon trout or lobster *mousse* to start; roast beef, lamb, or pork; apple turnovers or made-on-premises ice cream— are good buys. Dinner is à la carte and pricier. *First Class.*

SELECTED ENGLISH TRADITIONAL, INCLUDING PUB-RESTAURANTS

Anchor (Bankside; phone 407-3003), on the Southwark side of the Thames, dates to Elizabethan times. An engaging mix of clientele, both foreign and domestic, admire vistas of the City—there's an observation platform—across the water. Fare is pub-hearty; the ambience, history-laden. *Moderate.*

Antelope (22 Eaton Terrace; phone 730-7781) offers the economy of a pub in a smart Belgravia setting. Lunch upstairs on roast beef, Dover sole, or beef and kidney pie; downstairs buffet, too. *Moderate.*

Audley (41 Mount Street; phone 499-1843) is a Mayfair pub and offers a choice: Gilded Cage in the cellar, mainfloor pub proper, or Annie's Attick upstairs. All three are amusing and provide solid fare. *Moderate.*

Barley Mow (82 Duke Street; phone 629-5604) is handy to Oxford Street, not to mention Mayfair. A traditional pub, it's ideal for a lunch of, say, grilled sausages or pork pie and a salad. *Moderate.*

Bendicks (195 Sloane Street, near Knightsbridge; phone

235-4749) is at once a source of the fine chocolates bearing
its name and a tearoom-coffee house, small but inviting.
Moderate.

Blue Posts (6 Bennet St. at Arlington Street; phone 493-
3350) is an Edwardian pub just off St. James's Street and
popular with workers in the neighborhood, in part because it's an agreeable source of casual meals—dinner, as
well as lunch. *Moderate.*

Boswell's (239 Brompton Road; phone 373-3502) is not
going to win a beauty contest—the look is severe, with
meals served atop woven place mats surfacing coarse-
wood tables. But the ununiformed staff is friendly, and the
traditional English fare is straightforward. Concentrate on
chicken-mushroom and game pies and roast beef, saving
room for a fruit fool to conclude. *Moderate.*

Bunch of Grapes (207 Brompton Road; phone 589-4944)
is an unabashedly Victorian pub, with an attractive clientele and appealing, if conventional, pub-lunch fare. *Moderate.*

Carveries (Cumberland Hotel, Marble Arch; Strand Palace Hotel, Strand; Regent Palace Hotel, 12 Sherwood
Street, near Piccadilly Circus) are help-yourself-to-roast-
beef restaurants, at which a waitress serves you everything
but the main course, which you collect at a counter, with a
chef to assist, and with the happy understanding that you
may go back for more. Roasts of lamb (with mint sauce)
and pork (with applesauce) supplement the beef. Excellent
value. *First Class.*

Chelsea Potter (119 King's Road; phone 352-9479) lives
up to its location—smart, with a clientele of modish neigh-

borhood regulars, an engaging ambience, and good comestibles. *Moderate.*

Cheshire Cheese (145 Fleet Street; phone 353-6170): The
glory of the Cheshire Cheese is that it's tourist-proof.
There is not a locale in all of London more evocatively
Olde English. It has operated, as it proclaims, "under 15
sovereigns," beginning with Charles II, during whose reign
it was rebuilt. It occupies a building of its own at the corner
of the narrow street that leads down to Gough Square and
Dr. Johnson's House. Johnson was a Cheshire Cheese
habitué. His portrait hangs in a place of honor in the Coffee Room. Roast beef is the star of a traditional menu, with
all of the old favorites recommendable, most definitely including mutton chops. *Moderate-First Class.*

Dorchester Hotel Grill Room (Park Lane; phone 629-
8888): Extensive refurbishing elsewhere in this hotel notwithstanding, the Grill Room retains its somewhat unlikely, but agreeable, mock-Renaissance decor—coffered
ceiling, tapestried walls, red-leather chairs out of a King
Arthur movie—all very comforting. So, indeed, is the cuisine, an inspired meld of traditional English dishes, with
other specialties of the Cuisine Naturelle school, which
uses no cream, butter, oil, or alcohol. Beetroot and watercress soup with curd cheese and steamed stuffed leg of
chicken with tomato confit are typical *cuisine naturelle* of-
ferings. I am partial, however, to such British standbys as
rabbit pie, scallop *soufflé,* or Kentish pot roast, typical of
entrées on the good-value three-course lunch. At both
lunch and dinner, the opener is an oversize wagon piled
high with baked-on-premises breads in amazing variety.
Desserts—including sherry trifle and lemon syllabub—
are special, too. So is the old-school service. In my experience, one of London's best restaurants. *Luxury.*

Down's Wine Bar (5 Down Street, off Piccadilly; phone 491-3810) is skilled at preparing solid fare—coarse *pâté*, sautéed mushrooms, hamburgers—at tempting prices. Wine by the glass or bottle. *Moderate.*

English House (3 Milner Street; phone 584-3002) is just that: an elegant Kensington townhouse, antiques furnished, whose personable owner, Malcolm Livingston, serves traditional English dishes, mostly based on recipes from Michael Smith's excellent book, *Fine English Cooking.* The range is soused herring and chilled Stilton soup through fish pie, grilled home-made sausages, and mustard-baked chicken to maids-of-honor chocolate *pye* and hot apple crumble. Good-value table d'hôte lunches; dinner is pricier. In my experience, one of London's best restaurants. *First Class-Luxury.*

George Inn (77 Borough High Street, Southwark; phone 407-2056) is sufficiently venerable to be a property of the National Trust; it's the only galleried inn left in London. In the beamed tavern, a cold buffet is served at lunchtime. The dining room offers a set meal that invariably includes roast beef, as well as grilled fish and such traditional dishes as roast chicken with bread sauce. *Moderate.*

Grenadier (18 Wilton Row; phone 235-3074) is a pub that goes back to the early nineteenth century, when George IV was a customer. Clientele today is fashionable Belgravia. Lunches (and dinners, for that matter) are excellent, with decor on military lines—old uniforms, swords, and the like. *Moderate.*

Grove (43 Beauchamp Place; phone 589-5897) is a two-story pub with the bar downstairs—in warm weather, customers are out in front taking in the sun and the pedestrians. The restaurant above specializes in hot pies, grilled fish, and nice desserts. *Moderate.*

Hungry Horse (196 Fulham Road, at the end of an alley; phone 352-7757) occupies a pair of contiguous basement rooms in a Kensington townhouse. It's hardly fancy, but it offers delicious traditional favorites: smoked trout, leek soup, roast beef, steak, kidney-and-mushroom pie, double lamb chops. Delicious puddings and other desserts. *First Class.*

King's Head and 8 Bells (50 Cheyne Walk; phone 352-1820) is a venerable pub on a venerable Chelsea street, with the food as good (I know of no pub in Britain with more delicious grilled sausage!) as the look is handsome. Combine lunch with a visit to Thomas Carlyle's House nearby on Cheyne Row. *Moderate.*

Lockets (Marsham Court at Marsham Street; phone 834-9552): Origins are seventeenth century. The menu makes the best reading of any in town (they'll let you have it if you will but ask) and points out that Vanbrugh referred to it in his play *The Relapse*, which was the rage of the 1696 season and in which the character of Lord Foppington announces that he will "go to dinner at Locket's, and there you are so nicely and delicately served." You still are. Bill of fare is divided into Fore-Dishes, Soups (there is included at that point a venerable recipe for a potage known as Veal Glue), Fishes, Removes and Made Dishes, Grill and Side Dishes, and—on a separate card—Kickshaws (desserts, these), Savouries, and Cheeses. Start with potted shrimp, continue on to Cornish crab soup with brandy, following with baked English trout with bacon or jugged hare or venison, and conclude with brandy and sherry syllabub or Cambridge burnt cream, with a savory like mushrooms on toast for the last course. Clientele runs to MPs (Parliament is a neighbor). *Luxury.*

Maggie Jones's (6 Old Court Place at Kensington Church Street; phone 937-6462) is one of the most uncommonly good of the smaller London restaurants. Cauliflower soup to start; entrées like shepherd's or chicken-and-carrot pie; desserts like chocolate *mousse* or apple crumble; carafes of wine; homemade bread. *Moderate-First Class.*

Markham's (King's Road at Smith Street): The marvelously ornate Victorian facade of this busy pub is a neighborhood landmark, worth knowing about at midday, when its hamburgers and quiche appeal. *Moderate.*

Museum (Great Russell Street at Museum Street; phone 836-9213) takes the name of the British Museum, just opposite, and is indicated for a pub-lunch in connection with museum exploration. *Moderate.*

Porters (17 Henrietta Street; phone 836-6466) has quite the engaging old-time look that you expect in Covent Garden. Name of the game is hot pies—steak and mushrooms, chicken, even vegetable—with a sherry-soaked trifle most irresistible of the desserts. Fun. *Moderate.*

Richoux (Piccadilly, near the Royal Academy; Brompton Road opposite Harrods; South Audley Street at Adam's Row; and other locations, including New York City) is convenient for satisfying, albeit unpretentious, lunches, snacks, and dinners. *Moderate.*

Rose and Crown (2 Old Park Lane; phone 499-1980) is a convenient pub for a quick but relaxing lunch from the buffet at the bar—cold meats, cheeses, French bread, and the like, washed down with a pint of lager. *Moderate.*

Rules (35 Maiden Lane; phone 836-5314) has been a City landmark since the eighteenth century. Its heyday was during the reign of Edward VII when His Majesty was a customer. Look of the place—old prints, carved beams, massive silver serving trolleys, white-aproned waiters— could never be duplicated. If one sticks to standbys—roast Aylesbury duck, steak and kidney pie, mixed grill, grilled kidneys and bacon, filet steak—one does well. Go after the theater. *First Class.*

Samuel Pepys (Brooks Wharf, Upper Thames Street; phone 248-3048) is a modern pub-restaurant with more emphasis given to the restaurant than the pub. One drinks (and eats simply, if desired) in a bar on the ground floor; the high-ceilinged dining room—Thames view—is upstairs. Decor is neo-seventeenth century, the idea being to re-create the City's Restoration era, which Pepys chronicled in his diary. Fare runs to oxtail soup and roast beef. *Moderate.*

Savoy Hotel Grill (Strand; phone 836-4343): The problem with legendary restaurants is living up to the legend. None that I know is more successful in this regard than the Savoy Grill. Looks, to start: It's capacious, high-ceilinged, and traditional, albeit with light, bright touches. Staff, then: Maître d'Hôtel Angelo Maresca's team is as smiling as it is skilled and swift. And fare does not disappoint. The à la carte-only menu is just the right size—not over-ambitious but with more than enough to choose from. Traditional openers like smoked Scotch salmon, potted shrimps, or oysters on the half shell are good bets. Fish entrées—grilled dover sole or salmon trout especially— are superlative. So, for that matter, are mixed grills and lamb chops or such lunchtime plats du jour as Lancashire hot pot, shepherd's pie, or roast beef and Yorkshire pudding. And desserts! Skip them at your peril here, with the range blueberry tart and *crème brulée* through syllabub and Kenya strawberries doused with thick English cream. In my experience, the Savoy Grill is one of London's best restaurants. *Luxury.*

Shelley's (10 Stafford Street at Dover Street; phone 493-0337) is a strategically situated pub but steps from Piccadilly, whose restaurant is indicated for a stick-to-the-ribs lunch or dinner. *Moderate.*

Simpson's-in-the-Strand (100 Strand; phone 836-9112) was founded in 1828, was first rebuilt in 1865, and took on its current look—high-ceilinged, club-like—in 1904. You are not, in other words, going to be the first on your block. Indeed, the Savoy Hotels group, which has run this London institution for some time now, is fond of pointing out that it has thrived through eight reigns—starting with that of George IV. The hearty lunch or dinner you'll tuck into, might open with oxtail soup, embrace such trademark entrées as roast saddle of mutton, roast Aylesbury duck, steak-kidney-mushroom-oyster pie, or roast beef-cum-Yorkshire pudding. Apple pie doused with thick cream is the indicated sweet. Simpson's persists in the serving of an end-of-meal "savory"—Welsh rabbit; try it. And bear in mind that its trio of cheese standbys—Stilton, Cheshire, and Wensleydale—are first-quality. *First Class.*

Upper Crust in Belgravia (9 William Street; phone 235-8444) sports a crisp look in main-floor and basement dining rooms, with table d'hôte lunches its best buys, featuring entrées like fried chicken, roast pork, and beef sautéed in Guinness. Friendly. *Moderate.*

SELECTED SEAFOOD RESTAURANTS

Manzi's (1 Leicester Street; phone 734-0224) is an old-school seafood restaurant, with dining rooms on the main floor and in the basement, where the style is more casual, and there is counter service—worth knowing about, if you are alone. *Moules marinières* are very good, and so, for that matter, is the fish, Dover sole included. *First Class.*

Mr. Bill Bentley's Wine and Seafood Bar (31 Beauchamp Place; phone 589-5080) is amusingly conceived and with an attractive clientele. The bar is on the street floor, and the dining room, serving fish/seafood menu, is one flight up. *Moderate-First Class.*

Lucullus (48 Knightsbridge; phone 245-6622) is so easy to locate—next to Knightsbridge's landmark German Food Centre—that it's a good spot at which to meet friends. It's smart-looking, too—understated and in shades of gray. And the mostly Spanish staff is friendly. French-accented seafood is the specialty, but it can be uneven; Spain's rice-poultry-shellfish masterwork, *paella*, is more reliable. *First Class.*

Overton's (5 St. James's Street; phone 839-3774) is the kind of restaurant one sees in movies about fashionable London. Traditional specialty is seafood—lobster bisque, trout *meunière*, sole Overton's, *scampi en brochette*, fresh Scotch salmon, dressed crab. *First Class-Luxury.* (Note: Should you find yourself at Victoria Station, hungry and with time to kill, search out the Overton's branch near the entrance.)

Poissonerie de l'Avenue (82 Sloane Avenue, behind Peter Jones department store; phone 589-2457) is a worth-remembering Chelsea entry. Fish is fresh and prepared to order as you like it; ambience is light. *First Class.*

Scott's (20 Mount Street; phone 629-5248), with oversize, brown leather chairs at its central tables, and broad banquettes lining walls hung with sporting prints, is the epitome of the Mayfair eatery. Or, I should say, seafood eatery. The well-organized menu makes half a dozen concessions for meat eaters—including roast pheasant and partridge. But you go to Scott's for oysters and caviar, smoked salmon or trout, or an exceptional lobster bisque—among starters. And for such entrées as grilled Dover sole (which I recommend heartily) and such other fish choices as haddock, turbot, skate plaice, halibut, and lobster in a variety of styles. The waiting staff, mostly Italian, is swift and cordial. *Luxury.*

Wheeler's (12A Duke of York Street; phone 930-2460) is one of a venerable chain; Londoners who know the lot play their favorites. The delightful Duke of York Street Wheeler's occupies a building so narrow it comes close to not making sense. There is a dining room on each of the several tiny floors, and waiters negotiate the stairs and the compact areas with consummate skill. House specialty is oysters on the half-shell. There are a dozen lobster dishes, sole prepared in about as many ways, and sublime fried potatoes. *First Class-Luxury.*

Wiltons (55 Jermyn Street; phone 629-9955): It has, to be sure, had several locations. But Wiltons has been on scene since 1742, with seafood, game, and beef its specialties since the date of its founding. The current premises have been occupied only since 1984, albeit with furnishings from previous premises. Go for a lunch of, say, oysters or lobster bisque, followed by grilled sole, plaice, or turbot, or roast venison; with a traditional sweet to conclude—in the course of Jermyn Street shopping. *First Class.*

SELECTED FOREIGN RESTAURANTS

AMERICAN

Best of Both Worlds (Britannia Inter-Continental Hotel, Grosvenor Square; phone 629-9400) is, as its name suggests, only half-American. I'll let you discover the British specialties by yourself, but Yank favorites include shrimp cocktail with tangy sauce, potato skins with chili, New England chowder, Louisiana gumbo, tuna fish and chef's salads, southern fried chicken, pastrami on rye, Chicago franks, and Georgetown reubens. Are you ready? *First Class.*

Garfunkel's (57 Duke Street, Leicester Square, and a number of other locations) pleases with the likes of a menu running to hamburgers; pizza; and ice cream billed as American style, plain, or the basis of sundaes. *Moderate.*

Hard Rock Café (150 Old Park Lane, near Hyde Park Corner; phone 229-0382) is a stylishly decorated room absolutely loaded with Londoners—young, most of them—devouring the cuisine of their American cousins as though there were no tomorrow. Menu is limited: hamburgers and frankfurters pretty much describe it. But they're good, not always the case with our national staples in the U.K. *Moderate.*

McDonald's (Haymarket): We do not, heaven knows, cross the Atlantic for Big Macs, and I accord space to this McDonald's only because it's near theaters (indeed, framed playbills decorate the upstairs walls) and convenient for a precurtain burger that will tide you through to a proper postperformance supper. *Moderate.*

Parson's (311 Fulham Road; phone 352-0651) is indicated when you crave a hamburger. You may or may not like those to which Mexican embellishments like guacamole have been added, but *au naturel* and cum-cheese, they're tasty. *Moderate.*

CHINESE

Dumpling House (9 Beauchamp Place; phone 589-8240), though no relation to Dumpling Inn (below), might appeal, in the course of a Knightsbridge-area shopping bout, when the urge for Peking Duck overtakes you. Many Szechuan dishes, too. *Moderate.*

Dumpling Inn (15A Gerrard Street; phone 437-2567) is, to paraphrase one of Bette Davis's immortal lines, "a dump"—to look at, that is. It occupies a down-at-the-heels corner store in the Chinatown sector of Soho. If you are only two, you may have to share a cramped table, and, if the place is especially jammed, you may be directed to the basement. Regional specialty is Peking, and no matter what it is—pork or beef dumplings; scampi Peking style, grilled with garlic; shredded beef and green peppers; a dish of Chinese vegetables—it is delicious. The bill comes itemized in Chinese, so you end up trusting your hosts' abacus. *Moderate.*

Ken Lo's Memories of China (67 Ebury Street; phone 730-7734) stands out on two counts. First is ambience: The look is very sophisticated, indeed. Second is ownership: Lo is an eminent Chinese-born writer on the cookery of his native land, long resident in Britain. The name of the restaurant is a personal one: Dishes served, from various regions, are those he recalls from his youth and wrote about evocatively in a charming book, *Chinese Foods*. Order à la carte or table d'hôte. Lunch is cheaper than dinner, but the category is *Luxury*.

FRENCH

Au Bon Accueil (19 Elystan Street, off Brompton Road; phone 589-3718) is appropriate when taken in tandem with the nearby Kensington museums—or at dinner, for that matter. Ambience is light and bright; staff, attentive; fare, old-fashioned French. How about sautéed mushrooms, garlic scented, or eggs poached in wine as starters and *coq au vin* or braised wild duck as entrées? Desserts are hearty; wine, well priced. *First Class.*

Au Jardin des Gourmets (5 Greek Street; phone 437-1816) is just the Soho ticket for after-theater—and has been for something like half a century. The Jardin's métier is bistro food—onion soup and escargots, *entrecôte grillée* and lamb chops, sound salads, desserts that include a fabulous *crème brulée*, and well-priced wines. *First Class.*

Brasserie des Amis (27 Basil Street, opposite Harrods; phone 584-9012) is indeed a brasserie, and in the best sense: with stick-to-the-ribs French favorites—onion soup, escargots, steak French style, super salads. In addition, though, there are authentic Italian pastas. And service is at once agreeable and proficient. *Moderate*. (*Mes Amis*, a more formal restaurant, is directly next door, and another relative, *Relais des Amis*, is heart of Mayfair, on Curzon Street.)

Brasserie St. Quentin (243 Brompton Road; phone 581-5131) evokes its south-of-the-Channel counterparts at their classiest. This is a looker of a Gallic-staffed house, with downright delicious victuals—starters like quail eggs and whatever the potage du jour, through entrées based on duck or trout or beef. Have the mixed sherbets for dessert. Lively, lovely, and *Luxury.*

Capital Hotel Restaurant (22 Basil Street; phone 581-5171): By and large, everything is masterfully prepared and served, delicious to taste, and—given the ambience of the restaurant, relatively recently refurbished in exuberant traditional style by the skilled decorator Nina Campbell—enjoyable to eat. Crab bisque and chef's *pâté* are fine starters. Among entrées, *steak au poivre* and roast lamb are authentically Gallic. Salads, cheese, desserts, and wines are of equally high caliber. And the prix-fixe-cum-coffee, both at lunch and dinner, is sound value. *Luxury.*

Chelsea Room (Hyatt Carlton Tower Hotel, 2 Cadogan Place; phone 235-5411): You go to the Chelsea Room for the smart crowd (lots of neighborhood locals) and the smart ambience. It occupies beige-hued quarters up a flight from the lobby of a handsome hotel. Massive flower arrangements—calla lilies might be teamed with pussy willows and mums—are strategically positioned. You sit on Louis XV chairs upholstered in understated checks. Staff is essentially Continental, menu fairly standard Gallic with the occasional surprise—snails in a novel parsley sauce and fennel flavoring crab bisque, among starters; turbot in conjunction with lobster and cucumbers, and veal filet in a cognac-mustard sauce, grape garnished, among entrées. *Luxury.*

Hilaire (68 Old Brompton Road, a couple of blocks from South Kensington tube station and an easy walk from the Victoria and Albert Museum; phone 584-8993) is small and neat—it comprises main-floor and basement rooms in tones of gray and white, with bentwood chairs at the tables. The welcome may be tentative (most customers appear to be neighborhood regulars and the Anglo-French staff is shy). But the service is kindly and the fare creative. The well-priced three-course lunch might open with terrine of preserved duck and *foie gras*, continue with roast lamb served with a delicious onion compote and superb *pommes Dauphinoise*, and conclude with Hilaire's own rhubarb ice cream. *First Class.*

Interlude de Tabaillau (7 Bow Street; phone 379-6473): It's been a long opera or a full-length ballet at neighboring Covent Garden—and you've worked up an appetite. Relax over a sumptuous Interlude de Tabaillau dinner, opening perhaps with one of this house's celebrated *mousses*, later concentrating on a seafood or poultry specialty. Special sweets, an intelligently selected, predominantly French wine list, and expensive but fairly priced table d'hôte lunches and dinners. *Luxury.*

Langan's Brasserie (Stratton Street, off Piccadilly; phone 491-8822) is a two-story establishment, with the near-ballroom-size main-floor room the one to book for. Ambience is humming Art Deco, and waiters dart about in ankle-length white aprons, as they might in a trendy Paris bistro. Indeed, the menu is bistro inspired, essentially French, with delicious, no-nonsense openers like garlic-scented snails, *céleri rémoulade*, and hearty soups, followed by equally satisfying entrées, with choices of veal (*paillard de veau*), lamb (*gigot d'agneau*), or beef (*entrecôte grillée sauce Béarnaise*). French fries are masterful, likewise the potatoes styled *gratin Dauphinoise*, not to mention other vegetables like puréed spinach and glazed carrots. Have *poire belle-Hélène* or *baba au rhum* to conclude. And take advantage of the reasonably priced choice of French wines. In my experience, one of London's best restaurants. *First Class.*

Le Crocodile (38 Kensington Church Street; phone 938-2501): You've been doing the boutiques of Kensington Church Street, and you're famished. Pop into Le Crocodile for a French lunch that might embrace a hearty soup, roast pheasant, and the house's celebrated Grand Marnier *mousse* for dessert. Well-priced wines. *First Class.*

Le Gavroche (43 Upper Brook Street; phone 499-1826): A snazzy basement restaurant in Mayfair? Well, yes. And that is an understatement. Down you go to a subterranean chamber walled in green baize, its tables and banquettes oversize, with their floral centerpieces little works of art, their china delicate Wedgwood. An attentive Anglo-French staff, which seems to consist more of green-blazered captains than white-jacketed waiters, greets you with grins and brings crocks of sweet butter and baskets of *petits pains*, hard French rolls unsurpassed in London. With your aperitif comes a platter of *amuse-gueules*, exquisitely wrought canapés to gently ease hunger pangs. If you are prudent, you will have gone for the three-course-and-coffee-cum-*petits-fours* lunch. Each dish is brought by a pair of waiters, with a captain in attendance; one chappie lays the platter on the table; another, poof! removes its silver bell-cover. Cuisine is classically inspired but with Gavroche variations—a cream of crayfish soup flecked with caviar, or scrambled eggs with mussels in a kicker of a sauce, as starters; two species of fish from the morning's market bathed in butter-enriched champagne, or a rich *navarin*, or lamb stew, unlike any you have had in France. Desserts are masterworks—*mille-feuilles* in a warm vanilla sauce, the house's own sherbets, *soufflés*, and tarts. And the wine list just has to be the most extensive in the kingdom, with some bottles under £10, a few as pricey as £600. In my experience, one of London's best restaurants. *Luxury.*

Le Soufflé (Inter-Continental London Hotel, 1 Hamilton

Place; phone 409-3131) deceives with its Art Deco environment. You like the look—bright and perky red and white. But you don't quite expect an *haute cuisine* French restaurant. Then you watch the staff of pros at work, and then you taste the food. *Soufflés* are the specialty, cheese through chocolate. But everything is exceptional here—appetizers, like a delicate salad of breast of chicken and watercress dressed with walnut oil, through entrées like grilled veal escallop with lobster sauce, and on to carefully selected cheese in peak condition and a trolley full of baked-on-premises pastries. With an expertly collected cache of wines. Exceptional. In my experience, one of London's best restaurants. *Luxury.*

Ménage à Trois (Beauchamp Place; phone 589-4252) has achieved something of a reputation by limiting its repertory to first courses and desserts. Among the former, there are salads and terrines in abundance, with soups, as well. And the sweets are nothing if not original. Fun for lunch. *First Class.*

Truffles (Portman Inter-Continental Hotel, 22 Portman Square; phone 486-5844)—elegantly paneled, its picture-windows overlooking Portman Square—serves predominantly and deliciously French fare, often truffle accented and on Wedgwood bone china. Table d'hôte lunches and dinners are good value and built around such entrées as breast of duckling, filet of beef or veal, or grilled fish of the day, preceded by inventive appetizers, and concluded with memorable pastries or fruit desserts. *Luxury.*

GREEK

Little Acropolis (10 Charlotte Street; phone 636-8198) stands out—no mean feat in a neighborhood of Greek restaurants, west of Tottenham Court Road and the British

Museum. Start with a bottle of Greek wine (resin-flavored Retsina is available should you—like me—be partial to it). Continue with *dolmades* (rice-and-meat-stuffed vine leaves) or a mix of *meze* (super Greek *hors d'oeuvres*), selecting *moussaka*—the classic eggplant-minced-meat-cheese-sauced casserole—as your entrée. *First Class.*

HUNGARIAN

Gay Hussar (2 Greek Street; phone 437-0973) is a Soho destination of distinction, a first-rate Hungarian restaurant. To order here are all of one's favorites—chicken paprika, *gulyás*, stuffed cabbage, strudel. There are good Hungarian wines and engaging Magyar service. *First Class.*

INDIAN

Last Days of the Raj (22 Drury Lane; phone 836-5705), a title that will surely appeal to aficionados of the TV series "The Jewel in the Crown," does well by tandoori specialties—shrimp, as well as more usual chicken; this last-named turns up prepared in other ways, too. The menu is imaginative, by which I mean you want to conclude with one of the made-in-house ice creams. *Moderate.*

Khyber Pass (21 Bute Street at Sumner Place; phone 589-7311) is not going to win a beauty contest, but the fare is down-home Indian, curries on to other staples, and satisfying. *Moderate.*

Tandoori (153 Fulham Road; phone 589-7617) takes its name from the specially baked chicken that is perhaps the greatest culinary contribution the Moguls made to Indian cuisine. The restaurant features an authentic version of the chicken, with jumbo shrimp similarly prepared. *Moderate.*

(Note: Tandoori of Mayfair, under the same management, is on Curzon Street and a bit more costly.)

ITALIAN

Café Torino (189 Piccadilly, near Hatchards bookstore; phone 434-1921): It's been a busy morning in the shops, and you want a quick lunch. Café Torino is self-service, and if you don't think twice about the Italian city it's named for, you're apt to be surprised at how delicious the *lasagne* is. Non-Italian fare, as well. Bravo! *Moderate.*

Il Passetto (230 Shaftesbury Avenue; phone 836-9391) is indicated for a satisfying after-theater supper. Concentrate on typical dishes of the peninsula—minestrone, pasta, veal *scaloppine.* Italian wines. *Moderate.*

La Capannina (24 Romilly Street; phone 434-2473), on a typical after-theater evening, is quite possibly the noisiest restaurant in Soho. Which is going some. Food is tasty— *linguini al pesto,* for example, or the *saltimbocco alla Romana,* with chicken, seafood, and lamb dishes, as well. And excellent salads. *First Class.*

La Cucina (30 Rupert Street, Soho; phone 734-9415) is convenient after the theater, when you're hungry for a hearty pizza or a well-priced plate of pasta and a robust wine. *Moderate.*

Luigi's (15 Tavistock Street; phone 240-1795): You're hungry prematinee (location is Covent Garden, near theaters) or postevening performance. Luigi's—attractively old-fashioned to look upon, authentically Italian with respect to both staff and cuisine—may be just the ticket. *Stracciatella alla Romana* is the eggdrop soup quite as you remember it from Rome—or San Francisco. Ditto spaghetti *alla vongole, cannelloni, lasagne,* and *tagliatelle.* The *scampi* dishes are super, too. Ditto, the veal. A pleasure. *First Class.*

Sambuca (6 Symons Street; phone 730-6571) is a step from King's Road—modish and pleasant. Start with the hearty minestrone, and go on to pasta or a veal dish and possibly a dessert; they're good. *First Class.*

San Frediano (Fulham Road; phone 584-8375): Italian restaurants are a glory of gastronomic London; San Frediano is among the relatively new ones. The pastas are invariably reliable; so are meat entrées, most especially veal *scaloppine* in a variety of guises. *First Class.*

San Lorenzo (22 Beauchamp Place; phone 584-1074) is a mock-tropical garden—could the attempt, hardly successful, be to imitate Waikiki?—in a deep-down basement, whose waiters—decked out in jeans and blue aprons—are the least cordial I have encountered at any Italian restaurant in London. Menu is limited, but the food— minestrone among the soups, *fellucine* with a butter sauce, spaghetti with clam sauce—is not at all bad. Nor is the Sardinian house red, although a glass of it is quite the tiniest such I can remember being served. No credit cards. *First Class.*

Terrazza (19 Romilly Street; phone 437-8991) has an ebullient Soho buzz to it on both of its handsome stucco-walled floors. Order one of the chicken or shrimp specialties; a meal here is the ultimate Italian experience— delicious, hearty, animated. *First Class.*

Trattoria Imperia (19 Charing Cross Road; phone 930-8364) is unassuming but authentic, with a cheery staff, appetizing *antipasti,* fresh salad greens, and pasta cooked *al dente.* Okay for after-theater. *Moderate.*

SPANISH

Martinez (25 Swallow Street; phone 734-5066) is apparently ageless—and has been since it opened in the twenties. I don't know it for anywhere near that long, but for as long as I have, it has remained consistently good, occupying capacious quarters on a narrow, little street just off Regent. Authentic Spanish dishes—*paella,* of course, *calamares en su tinta, zarzuela de pescado y marisco, cazuela de merluza vasca, langosta en su aroma, arroz con pollo*—are reliable. Waiters must surely be the same engaging, courteous Spaniards who have been present since the opening. *Moderate-Luxury.**

SWISS

Swiss Centre (Leicester Square; phone 734-1291): There are four restaurants on the premises and a wide range, from *Chesa*—most costly of the group, with traditional specialties, fondue, *Berne platte, bundnerfleisch,* and the great potato dish called *rösti*—in a deluxe setting, to the quick-service *Rendezvous.* Decor is Swiss modern; service, Swiss efficient. *Moderate-First Class.*

LUNCH IN THE COUNTRY*

Gravetye Manor Hotel Restaurant (East Grinstead, Sussex, easily reached by frequent trains from Victoria Station to Gatwick Airport; thence, by taxi; phone 03422-810-567) went up in the seventeenth century and became

---

*See also The Ten Top Day-Excursions from London, Chapter 2.

known, in the nineteenth, for gardens created by the then-owner William Robinson and which, with trout lakes and woodlands, embrace the 30-acre setting of this establishment. In recent years, under the creative direction of owner Peter Herbert, it has become one of the most distinguished hotels and restaurants in the British countryside. The stuccowork and paneled walls of the sitting rooms are stunners. The restaurant is as good looking as its Anglo-French fare is delicious. You order from a carefully composed à la carte menu. Starters include cream of Jerusalem artichoke and scallop soup, home-smoked venison, or the house's wild duck terrine. Entrées run to grilled salmon and poached sea bass, sautéed breast of pheasant, lamb roasted Provençal style with herbs and garlic, and roast saddle of hare served with chestnut *purée*. The *Dauphinoise* potatoes are no better in southeast France, their area of origin. Choose among such sweets as carrot and hazelnut cake served with apricot sauce, pears poached in port, or walnut tart combined with praline ice cream and smothered with coffee sauce. And wines are superlative. In my experience, one of London's best restaurants. *Luxury.*

DEPARTMENT-STORE EATING

Barkers (Kensington High Street): *Terrace Restaurant* is on the second floor; *Rendezvous* cafeteria is in the basement.

Debenhams (Oxford Street): Descend to *Springle's Restaurant* in the basement, for lunch or tea.

Fenwick (New Bond Street at Brook Street) has both a third-floor, waitress-service restaurant and a basement cafeteria, for lunch, coffee, or tea on the run.

Fortnum & Mason (Piccadilly and Jermyn Street): The lower-level *Fountain*, on the Jermyn Street side, is eternally crowded and stays open late enough for after-theater sustenance and early enough for the service of breakfast. Besides sandwiches and cold plates, there are the famed Fortnum ice creams. Happiness of a summer sightseeing afternoon, I am here to tell you, is a chocolate soda with rum-raisin ice cream—and a blob of whipped cream for good measure—at Fortnum's. Alternatively, there is a café at the rear of the main floor; and there is, as well, the fourth-floor *Restaurant*—most serene and priciest of the trio, and with good paintings on its walls—for morning coffee, lunch, or tea. *Moderate-First Class.*

Harrods (Knightsbridge) offers a wide choice. Begin with the *Health Food Bar* in the food stalls on the main floor; continue to the *Dress Circle Restaurant*, up a flight, a self-service spot for coffee, afternoon tea, sandwiches, and pastries. Move to the fourth floor, where there are two restaurants—the informal café in the *Way In* department and the traditional-decor *Georgian Room*, with its own cocktail lounge and where one lunches very pleasantly, indeed. The Georgian Room's buffet afternoon teas are one of London's top values. Note also a winning pub, *The Green Man*, in the basement, ideal for lunch; and the *West Side Express*, with its own entrance and waffle-and-bacon breakfasts served as early as 7:45 A.M. *Moderate-First Class.*

Harvey Nichols (Knightsbridge) offers a green-and-white coffee shop-wine bar in the basement and smart *Harvey's at the Top*—on five. *Moderate-First Class.*

John Lewis (Oxford Street) has an attractive restaurant, reasonably priced and fully licensed, on its second floor; try it for breakfast, as well as later in the day. *Moderate.*

Peter Jones (Sloane Square) has a pair of eateries. The restaurant proper is à la carte, and the cafeteria on five affords fabulous views. *Moderate.*

Selfridges (Oxford Street) offers an extraordinary range: up-a-flight *Coffee Shop* (not only for lunch but for Devon-style cream teas in the afternoon); *Brass Rail* (for sandwiches and other hearty fare) in the main-floor food department; fourth-floor *Top of the Shop*—a vast cafeteria —and that same floor's waitress service, fully licensed, and most attractive *Grosvenor Room*; and, in the bailiwick that is Miss Selfridge's, the balcony coffee shop known as *The Bistro.* You may go broke in Selfridges, but you aren't going to go hungry. *Moderate-First Class.*

SUSTENANCE IN THE MUSEUMS

Most ambitious of the museum restaurants is that at the *Tate Gallery* (Millbank)—with an extensive menu (soups and omelets are moderately priced, but everything else is quite costly) and an extraordinarily long wine list. But you may opt to grab a bite at the pedestrian and adjacent *Café.* There's a self-service coffee shop at the *British Museum* (Great Russell Street). The cafeteria in the *National Gallery* (Trafalgar Square) has an express line for short orders and another queue for more substantial meals; it serves wine and beer. The restaurants in the *Museum of London* (Barbican) and the *Victoria and Albert Museum* (Cromwell Road) are bright and inviting, are open morning coffee through afternoon tea, and serve wine and beer. The self-service restaurant in the *Royal Academy of Art* is indicated for *pâté, quiche,* a sandwich, Ploughman's lunch, or simply pastry with morning coffee or afternoon tea; everything tastes good and the prices are right.

TEA AND DRINKS

Afternoon tea is no longer the occasion it used to be, not at least in busy, urban London. Country places are the best locales for the so-called cream teas—home-baked scones served with butter and jam and tiny pitchers of cream so rich it has to be scooped out with a spoon, not for one's tea but as topping on the scones. Still, that is hardly to say that London is without a number of especially inviting spots for an afternoon tea break. Decade in, decade out, the *Ceylon Tea Centre* (which has bravely resisted changing its name to Sri Lanka Tea Centre and is at 10 Irving Street, near Leicester Square) serves the best-value afternoon tea in London.

Department stores' restaurant facilities are evaluated above. Tea is particularly pleasant—if one can get a seat— at *Harrods' Georgian Room* (where the lure is an extraordinarily good-value buffet, with assorted breads-cum-butter-and-jam, cakes, and pastries galore), *Selfridges' Grosvenor Room, Peter Jones's Restaurant, Barkers' Terrace, John Lewis's Restaurant, Dickins & Jones's Restaurant,* and last but hardly least, *Fortnum & Mason's* ground-floor *Fountain,* main-floor *Café,* and fourth-floor *Restaurant.*

Hotels still remain the poshest tea spots. Tea is a special treat when taken in the ever-so-pricey *Palm Court* of the *Ritz* (Piccadilly)—sandwiches and cakes, with white-glove service to match. But there's a catch; you must book in advance. The *Dorchester* (Park Lane) is still another deluxe locale, and you get a little more to eat. At *Claridge's Hotel* (Brook Street), a splendidly liveried waiter will serve you in the lobby so that you can watch the passing parade. The *Waldorf Hotel's* (Aldwych) elaborately high-ceilinged lounge is a good tea locale when you're in the City (and features tea-dancing Friday through Sunday); but no more so, to be sure, than the not-far-distant *Savoy* (Strand). *Brown's Hotel* (Dover Street) has never been known to stint with the sandwiches and cakes in a wood-paneled lounge that is quite the most Olde English tea-venue in town. Still other hotels that I have enjoyed for tea are the *Hyatt Carlton Tower* (Cadogan Place), *Belgravia Sheraton* (Chesham Place), *Connaught* (Carlos Place), *Hyde Park* (Knightsbridge), *Cadogan Thistle* (Sloane Street), *Inn on the Park* (Hamilton Place/Park Lane), *Goring* (Beeston Place), *Britannia Inter-Continental* (Grosvenor Square), *Russell* (Russell Square), and—worth knowing about when you can't get a reservation at the Ritz (above)—its neighbors on Piccadilly, the *New Piccadilly*, *Athenaeum*, and *Park Lane*.

Cocktails can be congenial in the hotel lounges. I particularly like the dark-beamed bar of the *Connaught* (Carlos Place), the bright and lively cocktail bar of the *Dorchester* (Park Lane), the *London Hilton on Park Lane*, the *Inter-Continental London* (Hamilton Place), the *Savoy* (Strand), the *Hyatt Carlton Tower* (Cadogan Place), the *May Fair* (Stratton Street), *Claridge's* (Brook Street), the *Inn on the Park* (Hamilton Place/Park Lane), and the *New Piccadilly* (Piccadilly).

Pubs for drinking (as distinct from those earlier recommended for meals) are numberless. Those I have already singled out are eminently recommendable for drinking, as well as eating, purposes. Still, there are some others that I should like to call to your attention:

Black Friar (Queen Victoria Street, in the City)—with an opulent decor of mosaics and bas-reliefs.

Dirty Dick's (Bishop's Gate) boasts that it hasn't been

cleaned up in a couple of hundred years: spider webs are its trademarks.

Duke of Albemarle (Dover Street) is a well-located pub for the West End visitor in Piccadilly. Look is modish, drinkers likewise.

Lamb and Flag (Rose Street) is a theater-district landmark, a happy choice for after the play. This, the West End's oldest timber-framed drinking house, dates to the Tudor era.

Mayflower (Rotherhithe Street) is a half-timbered oldie named for the Pilgrims' ship, with a Thames view.

Piccadilly Nuisance (Dover Street) caters to well-got-up locals and drop-in visitors; pleasant.

Salisbury (St. Martin's Lane) is a between-acts drinks spot and an after-theater magnet, as well, with thespian types prevalent among the regulars. Look is opulent turn-of-century. Good eats.

Sherlock Holmes (Northumberland Street) is a monument to the fictional detective, with all manner of Holmesiana, even including an imagined mock-up of his Baker Street digs.

6

London To Buy

SETTING THE SHOPPING SCENE

The advantage of shopping in London is that, even though you're in Europe, it's all done in English. Sometimes, however, this is not an advantage at all; it's too easy, which can result in its becoming too costly. But shopping in the English language would not be all that worthwhile if there were not worthy wares. Not, mind you, that there are any bedrock bargains (except at the annual post-Christmas sales, when tabs can be rock bottom). Everything that is exported to the United States is, of course, somewhat cheaper on home ground, but usually not all that much, although the savings that can be effected when the whopping VAT tax is eliminated—about which I write in Chapter 7—can make purchasing costly items most attractive.

By and large, though, it is the design and quality and variety—and the smart way in which merchandise is displayed—that keeps us in stores for a disproportionately greater period of our time in London than should be the case if we want to see other aspects of the city than the insides of its emporia. Where to buy? Shopper's London breaks down this way:

Piccadilly—between Piccadilly Circus and Green Park. *First Class-Luxury.*

Regent Street—from Pall Mall to Oxford Street. *First Class-Luxury.*

Oxford Street—from Marble Arch to Charing Cross Road. *Moderate-First Class.*

Knightsbridge—including Brompton Road, Sloane Street, and Pelham Road. *First Class-Luxury.*

King's Road—Chelsea, from Sloane Square to Beaufort Street. *Moderate-Luxury.*

Mayfair—roughly, the area bounded by Park Lane, Regent Street, Piccadilly, and Oxford Street, and including Old and New Bond streets, Curzon Street, Savile Row, Mount Street, and Audley Street. *Luxury.*

Kensington—including Kensington Church and Kensington High streets. *First Class-Luxury.*

Strand and *Covent Garden*—from Trafalgar Square east, along with neighboring Covent Garden, splendidly refurbished as a shopping mall, facing St. Paul's Church. *Moderate-Luxury.*

PROFILING THE DEPARTMENT STORES

London's rank with those of the major American cities and a very few others—Tokyo, Copenhagen, Stockholm, and Paris. They are an effortless lesson in the capital's and, indeed, in the country's standard of living, the while reflecting British genius at marketing, merchandising, display, and salesmanship, not to mention taste.

Harrods (Knightsbridge) leads the pack, from the brilliant facade of its late nineteenth-century quarters through the merchandise and services of its four vast floors, with the extraordinarily stocked, tile-walled food halls, antiques, housewares (including garden equipment), and clothing departments outstanding, along with a variety of restaurants (including a handsome basement pub), barber shops, hairdressers, bank, theater-ticket bureau, and even a vet if you've a sick pet.

Selfridges is queen bee of the Oxford Street emporia, neoclassic, with a magazine and newspaper stand of exceptional diversity, exemplary food, London souvenirs, and china-glass-housewares departments, not to mention more places to eat than any other store.

John Lewis, Debenhams, and *Marks & Spencer,* the nationwide cut-rate chain, are among Selfridges' Oxford Street neighbors, with *John Lewis* the biggest and most impressive of this group (don't miss china and housewares in the basement). "Marks & Sparks," as Brits call it, is chock-filled with clothing buys.

Liberty, with its distinctive half-timbered facade, leads the Regent Street lineup; indeed, only Harrods is smarter. Liberty's celebrated prints, mostly paisley designs in silk and cotton, are made up into articles of clothing (beginning with neckties) and sold by the bolt; super housewares.

Dickins & Jones is Liberty's Regent Street neighbor with no standout features, as far as I can perceive.

Fortnum & Mason (Piccadilly) is eternally jam-packed with Americans, grabbing up its costly comestibles from tailcoated salesmen as though there were no tomorrow. It also offers a trio of restaurants and departments vending antiques (excellent), clothing, and assorted doodads.

Harvey Nichols (Knightsbridge) is a near-neighbor to Harrods, with pricey women's clothing, some men's, too; china and glass.

Barkers (Kensington High Street), recently refurbished and brightened up, is worth knowing about for its pharmacy, food, and china.

Peter Jones (Sloane Square) occupies an architecturally

striking pre-World War II building, but it disappoints within; Chelsea deserves smarter.

Army & Navy (Victoria Street) is convenient if you have need of a department store while in the area of Parliament, but it is, to this surveyor, the least interesting of the major department stores.

STROLLING THE STREET MARKETS

Petticoat Lane (Middlesex Street) is the most amusing, Sunday mornings, between nine and noon. Countless stalls line Middlesex and adjacent streets, defying easy classification: china and clocks, linens and luggage, jeans and jewelry, with the traditional whelks and cockles and mussels—old-time London's seafood favorites—always on hand, not to mention sandwich boards attached to grim-visaged elderly men, with the hardly optimistic intelligence to the effect that "The End Is at Hand."

Portobello Road is a two-part affair: flowers, fruit, and vegetables early weekday mornings; antiques—among a lot else—Saturday, the day long.

Camden Passage: hundreds of shops bulging with elderly—and really aged—objects, 10:30 A.M.–5:30 P.M. weekdays, with additional outdoor stalls open only Monday, Wednesday, and Saturday.

New Caledonia Market (Bermondsey Square): alfresco, Fridays only, from 7:00 A.M. until about 3:00 P.M., with some 250 vendors of antiques and assorted bibelots.

SELECTED SHOPS BY CATEGORY

Antiques: London is one of the great world antiques centers for seventeenth-, eighteenth-, and nineteenth-century furniture, ceramics, porcelain, maps, paintings, clocks, tapestries, and other objects, not to mention non-British antiques from France, Italy, the Middle East, and Asia. Besides the big dealers and auction houses, consider shops—often with good prices—on Knightsbridge's Brompton Road, Chelsea's King's Road, Kensington's Fulham Road and Church Street, and Portobello Road. To be noted, too, is the big, annual, high-caliber Antiques Fair, held for a fortnight in mid-June at Grosvenor House Hotel. *Mallett & Son* (New Bond Street), *Stair and Company* (Mount Street, along with a number of other Mount Street shops), and *Frank Partridge* (New Bond Street) are representative of the top stores, often with museum-caliber merchandise. There is a group of antiques markets—indoor affairs, with scores of dealers' shops—that are fun to browse and can yield important purchases, very often at good prices. These include *Antiquarius*, perhaps the best known, on King's Road; *Chelsea* (also on King's Road), and *Hypermarket* (Kensington High Street).

Shops with specialties are virtually limitless; some, to give you an idea, are *Aubrey Brocklehurst* (Cromwell Road), clocks and watches; *Bluett* (Davies Street), Oriental art; *S.J. Phillips* (New Bond Street) and *Eckstein's* (Jermyn Street), jewelry; *Spink & Son*, paintings, drawings, Asian art; *Hotspur* (Lowndes Street), English eighteenth-century furniture; *Valerie Wade* (Ebury Street), English nineteenth-century furniture; *Alistair Sampson* (Brompton Road), English eighteenth- and nineteenth-century furniture; *John Sparks* (Mount Street), Oriental porcelain; *W.G.T. Burne* (Elysan Street, off Brompton Road), glass; *Earle D. Vandecar* (Brompton Road), English porcelain; *Victor Franses* (Jermyn Street) and *Vigo Sternberg* (South Audley Street), tapestries; *Wildenstein* (New Bond Street) and *Arthur Tooth & Sons* (Bruton Street), fine paintings; *Weinreb & Douwind* (Great Russell Street), prints and maps; *John Jesse & Irina Laski* (Kensington Church Street), Art Nouveau and Art Deco objects; *London Silver Vaults* (Chancery Lane), silver.

Two stores with top-rank antiques departments are *Asprey* (New Bond Street) and *Fortnum & Mason* (Piccadilly). *Antiques Auction Houses* advertise their sales in advance, in the press; the range is wide—furniture, paintings, porcelain, old books and maps, silver, and carpets. Generally, sources of the merchandise are stated; these are usually estates of collectors. Contents of each sale are on view in the auctions rooms, usually two days before the auctioneer bangs his gavel. Often, there are illustrated catalogues of sales, obtainable in advance by mail at advertised prices. Major houses are *Sotheby's* (New Bond Street) —the largest and with overseas (including U.S.) branches; *Christie's* (King Street)—also in America; *Phillips* (Blenstock House, Blenheim Street, off Bond, and also in New York); and *Bonhams* (Montpelier Street, near Harrods).

Barbers (Men's) and Hairdressers (Women's): Choice barber shops include *Ivan's* (Jermyn Street), with a veritable platoon of barbers on two levels; *Michaeljohn's* (Albemarle Street); and the most atmospheric and Olde English of the lot (vending its own lime cologne, which is exported to the U.S.), *Trumper* (Curzon Street). Women's hairdressers include *Nevile Daniel* (Sloane Street)—should you want to have your hair done by the very same salon that sets the Queen's; and *Vidal Sassoon* (Sloane Street). Note, too, that there are big shops for both men and women in *Harrods* (Brompton Road).

Books: *Hatchards* (Piccadilly) has been my favorite source these many years, trip in, trip out; three floors and a very knowledgeable staff. *Foyles* (Charing Cross Road) is long-on-scene, as well, with vast stocks in limitless categories. *Heywood Hill* (Curzon Street) specializes in rare editions and will search out an elusive title. *Her Majesty's Stationery Office* maintains a diverse list, not unlike the U.S. Government Printing Office; main shop on High Holborn; others, kingdom-wide.

Cashmere and Other Sweaters and Woolens: *Westaway &* *Westaway* (Great Russell Street, opposite the British Museum) has extraordinarily diverse stocks and fabulously low prices. *S. Fisher* (Burlington Arcade): If my purchases are typical, Fisher's Shetlands wear and wear and wear. *W. Bill* (Bond Street) is a longtime favorite, too.

China and Glass: *Reject China Shops* (three detached shops on Beauchamp Place, another on Regent Street, branches in such unlikely cities as Bath and Oxford) is the ultimate bargain-china source; at any given time, you'll find diverse stocks of well-known English makers, along with assorted doodads—also cheap—including cork-based drinks coasters and place mats. *Jared* (Piccadilly) is long reputed for quality and diversity, very big on Spode, and reliable at shipping. *Chinacraft* (with outlets on Oxford Street, Brompton Road, Burlington Arcade, Regent Street, Beauchamp Place, and other locations) prides itself on having just about any pattern of any manufacturer. Don't forget department stores—not only *Harrods* and *Selfridges* but *Barkers, Peter Jones, Liberty,* and *John Lewis*, to name a few. And treat yourself to a perusal of extensive selections in such smart shops as *Thomas Goode* (South Audley Street) and *General Trading Co.* (Sloane Street).

Cheeses: *Paxton & Whitfield* (Jermyn Street) is long-established, with the quality as impressive as the quantity.

Chocolates: Most delicious sources include *Bendicks* (Sloane Street—also a tearoom), *Charbonnel et Walker* (Old Bond Street), and *Rococo* (King's Road). Food halls of department stores like *Harrods* and *Selfridges* have diverse stocks, as does *Fortnum & Mason.*

Clothing: The internationally reputed *"There'll Always Be an England" stores*—all of them unisex and costly—include *Aquascutum* (Regent Street), in my view, the smartest of the lot, and with a New York branch; *Burberrys* (Haymarket, Regent Street, and with their merchandise in their own and other shops throughout the planet); *Jaeger* (with half a dozen-plus stores in London: on Regent, Sloane, and Baker streets and Brompton Road, to name four)—most boutique like of our group; and, finally, *Simpsons* (Piccadilly) and *Austin Reed* (with its main store on Regent Street).

For clothes by well-known British designers like Jean Muir, Margaret Howell, and Zandra Rhodes, look in top department stores like *Harrods* and *Harvey Nichols*, but also in *Margaret Howell's* own shop (St. Christopher Place), *Zandra Rhodes'* own shop (Conduit Street); *Brown's* (a cluster of South Molton Street boutiques); the Beauchamp Place shops of trendy designers *Bruce Oldfield* and *Caroline Charles;* and *Fenwicks,* a multifloor clothing store on Bond Street that goes oddly underappreciated by transatlantic visitors (it has two good restaurants). The ubiquitous, Welsh-origin *Laura Ashley* has a number of shops; the one on Fulham Road is the main clothing outlet. Continental designers are strongly represented; France's *Cacherel* and *Daniel Hechter,* for example, are both on Bond Street. Finally, women's hats. You might enjoy an original from *Simone Mirman* (West Halkin Street)—milliner to both the Queen and the Queen Mum.

Men's clothes are very big in the first, unisex group of stores heading this category. So-called bespoke (custom) tailors are celebrated and include *Huntsman, Henry Poole,* and *Gieves and Hawkes* (Savile Row)—long established and with a traditional point of view; and more contemporary *Blades* (Burlington Gardens). *Moss Bros.* (Piccadilly), formerly a tuxedo-rental chain, has become an exemplary all-around clothier. *Kilgour French & Stanbury* (Dover Street) tends to be high style and pricey. *Bates* (Jermyn

Street) specializes in tweed hats and grouse-shooting caps, while *Lock* (St. James's Street) is the world's premier source of derbies, called bowlers in Britain. Haberdashers are at every turn. I am partial to three on Jermyn Street—*T. M. Lewin*, with super neckties, especially those of challis wool; *Hilditch & Key*, celebrated for its shirts; and ever-so-costly *Turnbull & Asser*, for both shirts and ties like no others in town and exported to the U.S. Of the department stores, *Liberty* and *Harrods* are menswear leaders; *Fortnum & Mason's* men's department is smart, especially for ties and cashmere sweaters; and *Marks & Spencer* is always worth exploring.

English Perfumes, Toilet Waters, and Soaps: *Floris* (Jermyn Street) and *Penhaligon's* (Wellington Street in Covent Garden, Brook Street) make their own, package them beautifully, and export them to America.

Engraved Stationery: *Frank Smythson* (New Bond Street) is known for its pale blue writing papers, but you may have white or ivory stock, as well.

Fabrics: *Liberty* (Regent Street): Fabrics by the yard—in traditional cotton and silk patterns—were the original stock in trade of this department store.

Flowers: *Joan Palmer* (Jermyn Street) has attractive flower arrangements, should you require a hostess gift, they deliver.

Jewelry, Silver, and Fine Gifts: *Asprey* (New Bond Street), *Garrard* (Regent Street), and *Mappin & Webb* (Regent Street) are full of beautiful things; no stores in town are more eminently browseable.

Kitchen Equipment: *Reject Shops* (Brompton Road) is to

kitchenware what *Reject China Shops* is to porcelain. Big stocks, small tabs. *David Mellor* (Sloane Square) has two floors full of the very latest and smartest objects. *Elizabeth David* (Bourne Street) writes beautiful cookbooks and sells beautiful kitchenware. *General Trading Co.* (Sloane Square) has extensive—and interesting—stocks. Again, don't overlook department stores, *Liberty* especially.

Linens: Try the department stores, *Harrods* and *Liberty* especially, but there are branches, as well, of the top two Italian linen chains—*Frette* and *Pratesi;* they're both on Bond Street.

Miniature Enamel Boxes: *Halcyon Days* (Brook Street).

Raincoats: *Aquascutum* (Regent Street) and *Burberrys* (Haymarket and Regent Street).

Scottish Tartans: *Scotch House* (Brompton Road and Regent Street)—with other Scots woolens and knitwear, including cashmere and Shetland sweaters; branches in Edinburgh and Glasgow.

Shoes: They can be found at every turn in this major shoe-producing country, but *Lobb* (St. James's Street) has long been celebrated for costly custom-made footwear, both men's and women's.

Sporting Equipment: *Lillywhites* (Piccadilly Circus)— with men's and women's sports duds, as well.

Toys: *Pollocks* (Scala Street)—which just has to be the world's loveliest old-fashioned toy store; adults love it.

Umbrellas: *Swain Aderley Briggs & Sons* (Piccadilly).

7

London To Note

ADDRESSES

British Tourist Authority offices in North America are at 40 West 57th Street, New York, NY 10019; 612 South Flower Street, Los Angeles, CA 90017; John Hancock Center, 875 North Michigan Avenue, Chicago, IL 60611; Plaza of the Americas, North Tower, Dallas, TX 75201; 94 Cumberland Street, Toronto, Ontario M5R3N3; and 409 Granville Street, Vancouver, British Columbia V6CIT2. Head office is at Thames Tower, Blacks Road, London W6. In London, take advantage of these sources of information: British Travel Centre (a joint venture of British Tourist Authority and British Rail, with information on London and all of Britain, as well as a train-ticket counter, money-changing service, and American Express branch), 4 Lower Regent Street; Tourist Information Centre (for all of England, including London), Victoria Station; London Visitor & Convention Bureau counters in Harrods department store, Brompton Road; Selfridges department store, Oxford Street and Heathrow Airport; Scottish Tourist Board, 19 Cockspur Street; and Wales Tourist Board, 34 Piccadilly.

BRITISH AIRWAYS

BA is the internationally respected national carrier; it began in 1924 as Imperial Airways and has evolved into the airline with one of the largest route networks in the world, flying to more than 140 cities in more than 70 countries throughout Britain, Ireland, continental Europe, the Middle East, Asia, the South Pacific, and Africa—not to mention Canada (gateway cities extend from Vancouver to Halifax). And last but hardly least, for the purposes of this book, the United States. No other airline has anywhere near as many gateways linking the United States with a transatlantic country; BA's 15 gateway cities are New York, Boston, Philadelphia, Washington, Baltimore, Anchorage, Los Angeles, Seattle, San Francisco, Miami, Tampa, Orlando, Detroit, Chicago, and Pittsburgh. Aircraft? Most transatlantic hops are aboard Boeing 747s and Lockheed L-1011s, with services in First, Super Club (Business), and Economy classes, as well as the premium-fare (First Class plus a surcharge) supersonic Concordes linking New York, Washington, and Miami with London.

The beautiful part of the Concorde is the fantastic rapidity of the crossing; cruising at twice the speed of sound, it traverses the Atlantic in three hours and 45 minutes. Departing on a morning flight, you take off before 10:00 A.M., Eastern (U.S.) time, enjoy an impeccably served, multicourse lunch aloft, clear Customs at Heathrow, take the bus or a taxi into town, check into your hotel, shower, dine leisurely by, say, 8:00 or 8:30 P.M., London time, enjoy a full night's sleep, and—on the morrow—no jet-lag. (Indeed, it's the elimination of jet-lag that has made the Concorde popular with regular business travelers to and from London and the U.S.; surveys indicate that 80 percent of the supersonic's passengers are in that category, with 70 percent of those repeaters, who appreciate not only the fast journey, but special Concorde services, including deluxe departure lounges in the U.S., separate check-in, and fast baggage pickup.) Which brings us to that all-important aspect of the operation of any airline: service.

I have never not known a smiling, superbly professional cabin crew on a British Airways flight, regardless of the class or, for that matter, the type of aircraft. (And I include domestic services in the British Isles—comprising, incidentally, shuttles, with meals and drinks served, linking London with Edinburgh, Glasgow, and Manchester.) And my hat is off, too, to BA ground personnel—invariably as congenial as they are efficient. (More airlines link the United States with Britain than with any other country. They include—to give you an idea—Air-India, Aer Lingus, Air New Zealand, American Airlines, British Caledonian, Delta, Icelandair, Kuwait, Northwest Orient, Pan American, People Express, Trans World, Virgin Atlantic, and World.)

BRITAINSHRINKERS

If you've precious little time to spare for out-of-London exploration, remember that Road 'n' Rail Tours operates a series of Britainshrinkers—day-long excursions to such points as Bath, Brighton, Cambridge, Cardiff, Stratford, and York, which include sightseeing (only selected sites) and lunch.

BUSINESS HOURS

Business hours are 9:00 A.M.–5:30 P.M., Monday–Saturday; however, some shops close Saturday at 1:00 P.M. Department stores, bless 'em, remain open Saturday until 5:30 P.M.; they have one open evening; I say "evening" rather than "night" because it's not very late—7:00 P.M. With Harrods (Knightsbridge), this traditionally has been

Wednesday. Oxford Street department stores stay open later on Thursday. Banks: Monday–Friday, 9:30 A.M.– 3:30 P.M.

CLIMATE

Milder than you may think and frequently drier, as well. Summer (June through August) averages in the sixties, with seventies as highs in July and August, and the occasional scorcher of a heat wave—say, maybe eighty— which throws the kingdom into a tizzy. (Because there is no real need for air conditioning, people feel the heat when it comes—especially British men, who do not wear summer-weight suits, which are usually unnecessary during the summer months.) Spring (late April and May) and autumn (late September and October) are generally fiftyish. Winter (November through March) averages in the low forties, although thirties weather is not uncommon in January or February. Northern England and Scotland can register somewhat lower temperatures the year-round. Moisture of some sort or other can appear at almost any time, not necessarily with notice; that is why Britons carry umbrellas as habitually as the rest of us do Kleenex. Raincoats—even in summer, which can be cool—are a convenience, too. This is not to say, though, that "bright periods," as the British weathermen call them, are all that infrequent.

CLOTHES

Dress as you would in any temperate-zone country, including your own. Men will want at least a tie or two and a jacket and/or suit for more formal occasions, like the theater, opera, concerts, or better restaurants; and women will want clothes correspondingly dressy for such times. During the day, in the course of exploration, be as casual as you like. The important difference with respect to Britain and North America is summer wear. There can, of course, be days that are scorchers when men will be glad to have a short-sleeved shirt and/or a lightweight golf or sport jacket of the kind we wear spring through fall in the United States and Canada. But gents do well to have along—even in summer—a sport jacket and/or suit and/or blazer of the weight we wear in winter at home. Women will feel comfortable the year-round with wool or wool-blend suits, sweaters, and the like, as well, of course, as lighter-weight dresses for hot days, which can also be worn under coats. And, if one's visit is any time from autumn through spring, a wool scarf and gloves are suggested for both men and women. Never, *at any time of the year,* should male or female be without a raincoat and a collapsible umbrella.

COURT CIRCULAR

The Court Circular is the daily bulletin issued by the Royal Household, as published in *The Times* and *Daily Telegraph* of London, the better to keep us posted on what the "royals"—as their subjects refer to them affectionately—are up to: dedicating hospitals, welfare centers, or schools; attending opera or film premieres; ribbon-breaking at new factories; visiting far corners of the planet; hosting (or being guests at) parties; mourning at funerals. Datelines are among the planet's most glamorous: Buckingham Palace, Windsor and Balmoral castles, Sandringham House, the royal yacht *Britannia*, for the Queen, Duke of Edinburgh, and Prince Edward; Kensington Palace (and Highgrove, their Gloucestershire house) for the Prince and Princess of Wales and their sons, Princes William and Henry (a.k.a. Harry); Kensington Palace, as well, for Princess Margaret (and her children, Viscount Linley and Lady Sarah Armstrong-Jones), the Duke and Duchess of Gloucester (and their children, the Earl of Ulster, Lady Davina Windsor and Lady Rose Windsor), and Prince and Princess Michael of Kent (and their children, Lord Frederick Windsor and Lady Gabriella Windsor); Gatcombe Park, in Gloucestershire, for Princess Anne and her husband, Captain Mark Phillips and their children, Peter and Zara; Thatched House Lodge, in Surrey, for Princess Alexandra of Kent, her husband, Angus Ogilvy, and their children, James and Marina Ogilvy; York House, in the St. James's Palace complex, for the Duke and Duchess of Kent (and their children, the Earl of St. Andrews, Lady Helen Windsor, and Lord Nicholas Windsor); and last, but hardly least, Clarence House and the Royal Lodge at Windsor (and occasionally the Castle of Mey, way at the northern tip of Scotland), for Queen Elizabeth the Queen Mother. (A member of the Royal Family who does not normally undertake royal engagements and whose name you will not often see in the *Court Circular* is the Earl of Harewood, first member of the Royal Family to be divorced—the present Countess of Harewood is his second wife—and a musicologist, whose seat is Harewood House in Yorkshire. He is a first cousin of the Queen, as the elder son of the late Princess Royal, a sister of the Queen's father, King George VI.)

CURRENCY

The pound is divided into 100 pence, written "p." There are 1p, 2p, 5p, 10p, 20p, 50p, and £1 coins; and there are £5, £10, £20, and £50 notes. You are still likely to come across old £1 notes and coins of the old pounds-shillings-pence currency; a shilling is the equal of 5p, and a florin—the two-shilling coin—equals 10p. As in every country, exchange rates are better in banks than from hotel cashiers.

Always have your passport along when you want to make a bank transaction, remembering that the bank-opening time is invariably 9:30 A.M. The banks usually close at 3:30 P.M. Some are open on Saturday mornings, as well. Note, too, that cashiers—even in many first-class hotels—unless as payment of a bill, will not cash guests' travelers checks, even in small amounts, as a simple courtesy of the kind extended by hotels of all categories the world over. (*Luxury*-category hotels *do*, however, extend this courtesy.)

CUSTOMS

ENTERING GREAT BRITAIN

If you've nothing to declare, as most pleasure visitors don't, walk through the "green" channel. (If you *do* have dutiable goods, walk through the "red" channel.) If you're traveling with no more than a bottle of spirits, carton of cigarettes, film only for your use, a camera or two, and neither narcotic drugs nor live animals, well, of course, you'll be passed right through—and with a smile. British Immigration inspectors are quite the politest I know, in any country. They convey the impression that no visitors they've ever met are more welcome than you.

RETURNING TO THE UNITED STATES

Each individual may bring back $400 worth of purchases, duty-free. That is allowable once every 30 days, provided you've been out of the country at least 48 hours. If you've spent more than $400, you'll be charged a flat 10 percent duty on the next $600 worth of purchases. Remember, too, that antiques, duly certified to be at least 100 years old, are admitted duty-free and do not count as part of your $400 quota. Neither do paintings, sculptures, and other works of art, of any date, if certified as original. It's advisable that certification from the seller or other authority as to their authenticity accompany them. Also exempt from duty, but as a part of the $400 quota, is one quart of liquor. And— this is important—there is no restriction on how much one may bring in beyond the $400 limit, so long as duty is paid.

DRINKS

The British drink large quantities of beer. The kind closest to ours is called lager, although hotel bars carry Danish, Dutch, and German imports. But the most popular beer with the British is "bitter"—either "ordinary" or "best." Another variety of beer is "mild"; when "mild" is combined with "bitter," the resulting concoction is called "mixed." Popular, too, is the rich brown brew called stout, made by Guinness and not unfamiliar to Americans. *Scotch whisky* is usually just plain whiskey in Britain, the nationality being implicit.

The upper classes have for long been quite serious—and knowledgeable—*wine* drinkers. Britain imports more sherry than any other land, and Britons drink considerably more sweet port after dinner than do the Portuguese, who make the stuff. They are very big on table wines, mostly French. They call red Bordeaux "claret" and German white Rhine wines "hock." Commonwealth wines are imported, too; best are the Australian reds. English *gin* is as good as Scottish Scotch. Drambuie, made with a Scotch base, is perhaps the best *liqueur* to come out of Britain.

Drinking is done in licensed restaurants, lounges, and theaters, not to mention hotels, where guests may order in their rooms even during hours when the public bars of the hotel must be closed. Drinking is also done in the British institution known as the public house, or *pub*, and known also—particularly in the case of those in residential neighborhoods—as the "local." These last-mentioned serve as social centers—for both male and female—for their districts. (Women's lib has long been commonplace in the British pub, where the barmaid is as prevalent as the barman.) Most pubs serve beers of but a single brewery (Ind Coope, Bass, Charrington, Courage, Watney, and Worthington are among the leading labels), which doubles as the landlord of these retail outlets for their product. Some pubs, though, sell more than one make of brew and are called "free houses."

Pub hours are worth remembering. Generally, pubs are open from 11:00 A.M. to 3:00 P.M. and then from 6:00 P.M. to 11:00 P.M., Monday through Saturday. However, on Sunday, they are open from noon to 2:00 P.M. and from 7:30 to 10:30 P.M.

ELECTRIC CURRENT

If you bring a shaver, hair dryer or blower, or iron, you'll need a converter gadget; U.S. department stores sell them. And you will also need a set of plugs with the various-size prongs to match the holes of outlets in London hotel-room walls (keep your fingers crossed!). The store where you buy your converter will be able to help you in this regard.

END-OF-YEAR HOLIDAYS

Christmas Day, Boxing Day (December 26), New Year's Eve, and New Year's Day—require advance planning, there being no British Rail service, as a rule, on the 25th (including trains linking Gatwick Airport and Victoria Station) and 26th and no overnight trains on December 31st and January 1st. Additionally, London's Underground and red buses do not operate Christmas Day and maintain curtailed schedules Boxing and New Year's days. Certain long-distance buses do not operate December 25. And the week between Christmas and New Year's sees certain ranking London restaurants and even the occasional better shop closed.

HOURS OF OPENING

Talk about individualists! In no country of the world with which I am familiar are hours of opening less consistent than in the United Kingdom. There is no national closing day for museums—as is the case with Tuesday in France and Monday in Germany, for example. Before you set out for a museum, art gallery, or open-to-visitors country house, check and *double*-check opening times.

LOCAL LITERATURE

Time Out, on sale each week at newsstands, is probably the most thorough of the what's-going-on publications, although *Where in London,* distributed free in most hotels (ask the hall porter) can be helpful, too. Of the newspapers, I consider the American-edited *International Herald Tribune*—available all over town—more useful on the Continent than in London, where it seems to me much more to the point for the English-speaking visitor to read the local press, which has the great advantage of being published in his or her own language. I regularly read *The Guardian* (most politically liberal of the quality national newspapers), the *Daily Telegraph* (most politically conservative), and *The Times,* the best of the trio to acquaint you with the ramifications of British eccentricity, as witness this, my all-time favorite *Times* personal ad:

IDENTICAL TWINS required to travel as social secretary/P.A. to English lady with large family, large house and big headache. Requirements: one of the girls must be able to type, have organized mind and speak French; the other to receive guests, supervise staff and generally organize house. High salary, an interesting life with much travel for the twins that fill these qualifications. Please write first with photo to . . .

And magazines: The Brits produce them beautifully and are as skilled and creative at typography and design as at writing and editing. I am partial to *The Economist*—a world-class news magazine; the long-on-scene *Illustrated London News*; *Country Life*—for its photos of beautiful debutantes; *Harpers & Queen*, British *Vogue*, and British *House & Garden*; and magazines of the national Sunday newspapers—*Observer, Sunday Times,* and *Daily Telegraph*.

MONARCHS

After that of our own country, we know British history better than that of any other land. Indeed, I will wager that Americans can more easily rattle off the names of Britain's nineteenth-century monarchs than they can the names of American nineteenth-century presidents. At this point, let me capsulize—to the bare bones, for quick reference as you travel—the reigns of English (and, later, British) monarchs, beginning with the sainted Edward the Confessor (who began the rebuilding of London's Westminster Abbey as we see it and whose reign was followed, within a year, by the Norman Conquest). Years given indicate the duration of each sovereign's reign:

Edward the Confessor • 1042–1066
Harold • 1066
House of Normandy
William I (the Conqueror) • 1066–1087
William II • 1087–1100
Henry I • 1100–1135
House of Blois
Stephen • 1135–1154
House of Plantagenet
Henry II • 1154–1189
Richard I • 1189–1199
John • 1199–1216
Henry III • 1216–1272
Edward I • 1272–1307
Edward II • 1307–1327
Edward III • 1327–1377
Richard II • 1377–1399
House of Lancaster
Henry IV • 1399–1413
Henry V • 1413–1422
Henry VI • 1422–1461
House of York
Edward IV • 1461–1483
Edward V • 1483
Richard III • 1483–1485
House of Tudor
Henry VII • 1485–1509
Henry VIII • 1509–1547
Edward VI • 1547–1553

Mary I • 1553–1558
Elizabeth I • 1558–1603
House of Stuart
James I (of England, and VI of Scotland) • 1603–1625
Charles I • 1625–1649

[Commonwealth rule of Oliver Cromwell and Richard Cromwell]
House of Stuart
Charles II • 1660–1685
James II • 1685–1688
William III and Mary II • 1689–1702
Anne • 1702–1714
House of Hanover
George I • 1714–1727
George II • 1727–1760
George III • 1760–1820
George IV • 1820–1830
William IV • 1830–1837
Victoria • 1837–1901
House of Saxe-Coburg
Edward VII • 1901–1910
House of Windsor
George V • 1910–1936
Edward VIII • 1936
George VI • 1936–1952
Elizabeth II • 1952–

PASSPORTS

Passports are necessary for admission to Great Britain and must be presented to U.S. Immigration upon your return. Apply at U.S. Department of State Passport Offices in major cities (look under U.S. Government in the telephone directory) or—in smaller towns—at the office of the clerk of a federal court and, as long as the practice obtains, at certain post offices. Allow four weeks, especially for a first passport (valid for ten years), for which you'll need a pair of two-inch-square photos, proof of identity, and a birth certificate or other proof of citizenship. There's a $42 fee (subject to change) for first passports; renewals—also valid for ten years—are cheaper. If you're in a hurry when you apply, say so; Uncle Sam will usually try to expedite. Upon receipt of this valuable document, sign your name where indicated, fill in the address of next of kin, and keep it with you—*not packed in a suitcase*—as you travel. In case of loss, contact local police, United States Embassy (Grosvenor Square, London), or Passport Office, Department of State, Washington, DC 10524.

STEAMSHIP SERVICE

Transatlantic steamship service is almost—but not quite—ancient history. Cunard Line's *Queen Elizabeth* 2 valiantly maintains scheduled sailings—about a dozen per year—between New York and Southampton, with certain of the westbound crossings stopping also at the French port of Cherbourg (see *France at Its Best* and *Paris at Its Best*) en route to New York. Cunard, in tandem with British Airways, offers a good-value fly-one-way (via the supersonic Concorde), sail-the-other (via the *QE2*) package.

TELEPHONES

What is important to remember, in the case of public phones, is that you don't insert the money until you have dialed your number and heard a rapid *peep-peep* signal. With the advent of the peep-peeps, plunge your coin into the slot, and, when your party has answered, you are ready to communicate. The busy signal is not all that different from our own, albeit a little higher pitched. If you have problems, dial 100 for help; dial the same number if you want to call collect, using the term "reverse charge." Information is 192 in London and throughout Britain. Be careful about transatlantic calls from hotel rooms; service charges made by the hotel can be outrageous. If you do call home from your hotel room, make it collect; otherwise, call from a public booth or a post office, unless your name is Daddy Warbucks. That said, let me note a fairly priced transatlantic phone scheme. It's called *Teleplan*, and a limited number of hotels offer it; those of Hilton International have pioneered the plan, which is a service of AT&T.

THE TIME

Great Britain is on Greenwich mean time, five hours ahead of eastern standard time in the United States. Add an additional hour's difference each for central, mountain, and Pacific U.S. zones. Clocks in Britain are advanced one hour from about mid-April to mid-September, when the country goes on "summer time."

TIPPING

Generally, restaurants and cafés do not add a service charge; tip 15 percent. Tip bellhops and baggage porters nominally; likewise, doormen, for getting you a cab. Tip hall porters—that's English for concierge—*only* if they've performed special services for you during your stay. (Handing you your key is not a special service.) Tip taxi drivers 10 to 15 percent. Barbers and hairdressers get 10 percent, or more—up to 15 percent—if they've done a super job and the shop is a fancy one. Barmen in pubs are not tipped for the drinks they serve clients at the bar; tip only for service at tables.

TOURS, TOUR OPERATORS, TRAVEL AGENTS

Agents, first: select one who is affiliated with the American Society of Travel Agents (ASTA) and, preferably, who knows Britain first hand. For an initial trip, some travelers are happy with the convenience of a package. Operators making a particular specialty of Britain—whose packages may be booked through retail travel agents—include Abercrombie & Kent, Air-India Tours, British Airways Tours, Cosmos Tours, Esplanade Tours, Frames, Great Britain Vacations Division of CIE Tours, Globus Gateway, Maupintour, Pan American Airways' Holidays, Trafalgar Tours, Travcoa, and TWA Getaway Tours.

VAT

VAT is the British national sales tax, a 15 percent levy on goods, as well as services, such as hotel rooms and meals, in which cases it must, according to British law, be included—along with service charges—in quoted prices. Note, though, that with fairly substantial purchases in stores—the minimum was £60 at time of writing but is subject to change—you may arrange to have the amount of the VAT refunded to you by mail to your home address by the seller who provides you with a certification of your purchase, which you present to British Customs (showing your purchase) upon leaving the United Kingdom. At that point, the Customs-authenticated form is posted to the seller who, usually in a matter of weeks, dispatches your refund to you in the form of a pounds-sterling check that your bank will convert to dollars, charging a fee in the process. Complicated? You bet!

_____ INCIDENTAL INTELLIGENCE _____

Airports

Heathrow Airport is 14 miles from town, making taxis a fairly expensive proposition; buses into town run frequently, and they're cheap and efficient. *Gatwick Airport* is more distant from the city, but, to compensate, is linked with it by rapid, comfortable, and frequently departing trains to and from Victoria Station.

Railway Stations

London has more than a dozen railway stations—surely it sets a world record among cities in this respect—so it is essential to understand clearly where you'll be departing from. Of this large group of terminals, the most important are *King's Cross* (trains to the north, through to Edinburgh), *Euston* (trains to the north, through to Glasgow, and boat trains to Ireland via Liverpool), *Charing Cross* (with trains mainly for the southeast), *Liverpool Street* (trains heading east and northeast), *Paddington* (for west and southwest points), *Waterloo* (south), and *Victoria* (southern points and the Continent).

Public Transportation

Public transportation is excellent. The subway—officially the *Underground*, but also known as the Tube—is one of the best such systems in the world; free route maps of the system are available from ticket-sellers at every station. The Underground embraces eight major lines, each of whose routes has a color of its own on the system maps. Ascertain the Underground station nearest to your destination, determine which line it is on, and plot your route by means of the system map, noting whatever transfers en route may be necessary. The stations indicated by big circles on the map as "Interchanges" are where you may transfer to connecting lines. There is only one class of travel, with fares determined by the length of the trip. You announce your destination to the ticket agent when purchasing your ticket, and he or she will tell you the amount of your fare. Remember to hold on to your ticket for surrender at journey's end. And remember, too, that Underground ticket agents and conductors are invariably helpful. If at all in doubt about your trip—particularly if you will have transfers to make en route—don't hesitate to ask for help.

Buses can be a more complicated matter. But the stops on each route are clearly listed at each and every bus-halt. Among routes traversing central London (with some major stops indicated): *Route 9* (Kensington High Street, Knightsbridge, Hyde Park Corner, Piccadilly, Trafalgar Square, Aldwych, St. Paul's); *Route 11* (King's Road, Sloane Square, Buckingham Palace Road, Whitehall, Trafalgar Square, Aldwych, St. Paul's); *Route 14* (Fulham Road, South Kensington, Brompton Road, Knightsbridge, Hyde Park Corner, Piccadilly Circus, Shaftesbury Avenue, Tottenham Court Road); *Route 74* (Earl's Court, South Kensington, Knightsbridge, Hyde Park Corner, Marble Arch, Baker Street, Regent's Park Zoo); *Route 88* (Bayswater Road, Marble Arch, Oxford Circus, Piccadilly Circus, Trafalgar Square, Whitehall, Tate Gallery). Bus fares are calculated by distance. You board from the rear, seat yourself either on the main level or upstairs (where you may smoke). Simply state your destination to the conductor when he or she approaches and pay the requested amount, retaining the ticket you are given, in case you are later asked to produce it. Bus conductors—traditionally Cockney and either male or female—are now West Indian and East Indian, as well. Like their Underground colleagues, they are the traveler's best friends in London; feel free to ask their counsel. If your stay in London will be lengthy, consider purchasing Underground and/or Bus passes, which are available for varied periods of time.

Taxis are especially designed as taxis, with plenty of leg room and headroom so that it's easy to stretch out and easy to step in and out; they are the most civilized such conveyances of any country on the planet. They are metered, but nominal extra charges are made for luggage, and drivers are tipped 15 percent. They may be hailed as they pass or picked up at taxi-ranks, of which there are many. Taxi-ranks have phones; two worth knowing are St. George's Square (834-1014) and Sloane Square (730-2664). The phone for All-London Radio Taxis is 286-4848. Hotel doormen are expert at securing taxis, and you need not be a guest at the hotel to ask the doorman's help in this regard; naturally, he will expect a tip for his service.

Self-drive cars are obtainable from a great number of firms. The two American leaders, *Avis* and *Hertz*, are both on the scene, but so are many English firms, of which *Godfrey Davis* and *J. Davy* are among the best known.

Private escorted sightseeing: Several firms specialize in tailor-made touring. One such, *Grosvenor Guide Service* (30 Harwood Road, London SW6; phone 736-9779), is operated by the knowledgeable Judy Hoade and a staff of sophisticated, attractive women, all of them trained and licensed guides. Mrs. Hoade or one of her colleagues will take you where you want to go; they use their own cars and act as guide-drivers. If you like, they'll come up with imaginative suggestions for excursions—shopping in town, inspecting an Inn of Court with one of its members, and lunching with him in that Inn's Great Hall; touring Parliament with an insider, privately; taking in Royal Ascot or a polo match at Windsor Great Park.

Tour operators run a variety of sightseeing tours by bus, both of London proper and of attractions nearby and longer excursions, as well. These include *American Express* (Haymarket), *Frames* (Herbrand Street), and *London Transport* (Broadway).

London is eminently walkable by oneself, map in hand. But there are organized *walking tours* of the various sections of town. Contact *London Walks* (Conway Road) or *Discovering London* (Pennyfield's, Brentwood, Essex).

London and environs from the Thames is eye-filling and easily undertaken by means of scheduled river boats, during the warm-weather months. Launches depart from Westminster and Charing Cross piers, to such points as Hampton Court, Kew, and Greenwich. Ask *Thames Passenger Services* (Charing Cross Pier, Victoria Embankment) for details.

London Addenda

Besides the banks, there are change bureaus at Victoria Station (Thomas Cook) and such department stores as Harrods, Selfridges, and Barkers, among others. If you hold an American Express credit card and need money, present it at *American Express* offices on Haymarket and on Brompton Road, opposite Harrods. The *Trafalgar Square Post Office* (William IV Street) is open from 8:00 A.M. to 8:00 P.M. Monday through Saturday, and 10:00 A.M. to 5:00 P.M. Sundays and Bank holidays. The *London Taxi Lost & Found* is at 15 Penton Street. The *All-Purpose Emergency Telephone Number*—for police, fire, and ambulance—is 999. You may dial it from any telephone—and for free; no coin is necessary. Dial 246-8041 for the *London Visitor & Convention Bureau's* daily recorded roundup of visitor attractions; dial 730-3488 for answers to specific questions by the Bureau. *London Transport's* phone number—for information on the Underground and buses—is 222-1234, round-the-clock. *American Embassy* (including Consulate

General and Commercial Attaché) is on Grosvenor Square (phone: 499-9000). *Canadian High Commission* is at Canada House, Trafalgar Square (phone: 930-9741). And, lastly, the weather. Dial 246-8091 for the latest prediction.

8

The Britain Beyond London

Day-long excursions—I delineate what I consider to be the top ten, to be undertaken from the capital, in Chapter 2—are but frosting on the cake. It is no longer enough to fly the Atlantic to be dazzled by the Crown Jewels in the Tower, the Elgin Marbles in the British Museum, the eerily visionary Blake paintings at the Tate Gallery—and fly back. Ideally, one begins and ends in London. With exploration of the provinces in between. It is long since time to appreciate that British trains are comfortable; British highways, advanced; British provincial hospitality, exemplary; and—certainly for those of us from enormous North America—British distances, relatively short.

There is no longer any excuse for touristic timidity in this land, especially when one considers that some 49 million of the 56 million Britons live beyond London. I make my case for exploration of the kingdom, John o' Groats to Land's End, in 28 tightly packed chapters of this book's companion volume, *Britain at Its Best*. Herewith, allow me to capsulize distinctive attributes not only of provincial

England, but also of northerly Scotland and easterly Wales, as well—with the hope that you will consider extending your London stay into a beyond-the-capital journey, or failing that, plan for a return engagement that will see you survey those segments of the kingdom that strike your fancy.

SOUTH OF LONDON

Geographically southerly, London lends itself not only to such day-long excursion points as Brighton, Salisbury, and Winchester (see Chapter 2), but also to in-depth exploration. Indeed, no region of Britain is more generously endowed with worthwhile destinations, the range a cluster of islands that are closer to the coast of France than to that of England, to underappreciated port cities and a gentle countryside dotted with treasure-laden stately homes.

CHANNEL ISLANDS

The Channel Islands are part of the British Isles but not part of the United Kingdom. They owe allegiance to the Queen as Commonwealth members, but they are self-governing. They date to the period following the Norman Conquest in 1066. Two centuries later, when continental Normandy, of which they were a part, was politically detached from England, the islands chose to remain with the English Crown; and so they did, by means of constitutions granted by King John still in effect. Save for defense and foreign affairs—in British hands—they govern themselves; each of the two major islands has its own parliament—called the States—and crown-appointed head of state, or Bailiff. Blessed with a milder climate than that of the mainland and with duty-free shopping without the 15 percent VAT tax imposed in the U.K., they lure masses of British vacationers spring through fall.

Transatlantic visitors go less for sun and sand than for exploring a bit. Which islands? Both majors have a principal town-cum-picturesque harbor. Beyond, in the countryside (yes, you *will* see Jersey cows on Jersey, Guernsey cows on Guernsey), idyllic beaches lie beneath rocky cliffs or tuck themselves into neat coves.

Jersey, nine miles long by five miles wide, bases itself on St. Helier, the capital, edging a natural harbor on the south coast, and it is at its most impressive in and about Royal Square, flanked by the elegant little States, or Parliament, and the also-impressive Royal Court, with pedestrians-only King Street leading from it. The *Jersey Museum's* big draw is a room celebrating locally born actress Lillie Langtry ("The Jersey Lily") and a mistress of King Edward VII. *Fort Regent* is a surprisingly massive leisure complex. And beyond St. Helier, lures include a picture-book fortress, *Mont Orgueil;* the *German Military Underground Hospital,* from the World War II period when the islands were Nazi-occupied; and author Gerald Durrell's *Jersey Wildlife Preservation Trust,* whose residents are endangered animal species, such as gorillas, orangutans, and snow leopards.

Guernsey: Quieter Guernsey's chief town, St. Peter Port, is even more picturesque than St. Helier. A mix of Georgian, Regency, and Victorian architecture, it straddles a horseshoe of a hill that encloses a boat-dotted harbor, with Gothic-era *Town Church,* eighteenth-century *Royal Court House* (both Parliament and courthouse), and shop-lined High Street all nearby. Beyond, in the countryside, are *Maison Victor Hugo,* where the French author lived in mid-nineteenth-century exile; the *Guernsey Museum and Art Gallery;* and thirteenth-century *Castle Cornet.*

Dover and the Stately Homes of Kent

Dover: Canny Romans were the first to appreciate Dover's situation as the English Channel port providing the shortest sea-crossing to continental Europe. Indeed, a Roman-constructed lighthouse remains as a remnant of five Channel towns united as the Cinque Ports in a joint coastal defense effort (and to this day confederated under an honorary Lord Warden). Dover's location—adjacent to its landmark White Cliffs, the closest bit of Britain to France—has always made it special. Monarchs, from Henry VII onward, contributed to its development as a harbor and a bastian of defense. *Dover Castle* straddles a chalky cliff that backs the town and port, built around a twelfth-century keep, protected by magnificent walls, with a tiny Romanesque chapel its jewel. Down below, modern Dover's seafront is edged by *Marine Parade* and the *Eastern Docks* from which car ferries link England with French, Belgian, and Dutch ports. *Shakespeare Cliff* rises 350 feet skyward, to the west. And on the town's High Street is *Maison Dieu,* the thirteenth-century town hall, its Council Chamber lined with paintings of sovereigns associated with the town (including Queen Elizabeth I and Queen Anne) and lord wardens of the Cinque Ports (including Sir Winston Churchill and the first Duke of Wellington).

Kent's country houses are among the kingdom's most important. *Chartwell,* though dating only to the Victorian era, was the country home of Sir Winston Churchill and his family for four decades, and it brims with Churchilliana—Churchill's paintings, a memento-filled study, and the Museum Room with, among much else, a letter from President Franklin D. Roosevelt, in which FDR extends support to his friend at a time—June 1941—when Britain was still fighting World War II alone, half a year before the U.S. entered the conflict. *Knole,* built in the fifteenth century, is the textbook prototype of the early English stately home. It sprawls over a multiacre tract, a maze of vast courts, steep-chimneyed roofs, towers, gables, turrets, and three notable rooms—galleried Great Hall, Venetian Ambassador's bedroom, and Brown Gallery, filled with Old Master paintings. *Penshurst Place,* not unlike Knole, is Tudor and turreted, with a later, resplendent Long Gallery its most opulent interior space. *Igtham Mote,* though small and relatively simple, is significant in that it is one of the rare remaining English houses surrounded by a water-filled, swan-populated channel. And both *Hever Castle* and *Leeds Castle* have strong royal associations, in both cases revolving around Henry VIII.

SOUTHAMPTON AND THE SOUTH COAST

Given its situation—on the body of water called the Solent, facing the English Channel, but with the Isle of Wight positioned before it as a welcome natural obstruction against nasty weather—it is hardly surprising that Southampton was singled out for maritime prowess as early as the start of the Christian era. William the Conqueror's successors developed a port of consequence. And New World visitors want to remember that the Pilgrims first set sail from Southampton in April of 1620, with their intermediary stop in Plymouth necessitated because the *Mayflower's* then-sister ship needed repairs. A monument commemorates the seventeenth-century event, and a nearby plaque honors the two million U.S. troops who sailed from Southampton after D-Day, 1944.

The marvel of the city is its felicitous rebuilding, following World War II bombing. Requisite destinations are *Southampton Art Gallery,* one of the very best in medium-size British cities, Italian Renaissance Old Masters through French Impressionists; *Tudor House,* half-timbered and now a museum delineating the city's history; and *Wool House,* medieval in origin and now a maritime museum.

Nearby *Portsmouth* is Southampton's major urban rival, not—in my view—as well rebuilt after World War II as Southampton, but with a trio of smashing lures. *H.M.S. Victory* was the ship on which Lord Nelson—hero of the Battle of Trafalgar, during which the fleets of France and Spain were vanquished and Napoleon along with them—was fatally wounded in 1805, and on which, today, sailors and Marines take visitors about, stem to stern. The *Royal Naval Museum*, just opposite, brims with Nelsoniana and other exhibits that bring to life the British Navy's history. Adjacent, also, is the extraordinary *Mary Rose Exhibition*, occupying an eighteenth-century boathouse, with more than 6,000 objects recovered only in recent years from the long-wrecked *Mary Rose*, a warship commissioned by Henry VIII.

An agreeable boat ride from Southampton, the 13 mile by 23 mile *Isle of Wight* is visitable for two principal monuments. Foremost is *Osborne House*. Prince Albert, Queen Victoria's talented consort, had a major hand in its design; it evokes a multitowered Italian Renaissance villa with much charm. And its interiors—quite literally Victorian—are just as Her Majesty left them when she died in her Cowes bedroom. The State Drawing Room's floor is embedded with a brass plaque bearing the legend: "Here in Peace Queen Victoria Lay in State Awaiting Burial at Windsor, 1 February 1901." Osborne House's major visitor-competition is *Carisbrooke Castle*. Charles I stayed there for a year, in the course of what was intended as his escape from Hampton Court Palace, outside London. The medieval castle—moated and with a drawbridge—contains a pair of chapels and the island's historical museum.

CHICHESTER AND RYE IN SUSSEX

The earlier-counseled day's excursion to Brighton—Sussex's most celebrated town—does not allow for other regional treats.

Chichester, for example, is the site of an annual May–September arts festival that's among Britain's most popular. Equate Chichester with charm. Its sixteenth-century Market Cross straddles the intersection of the four principal streets—North, West, South, and East. Nearby *Chichester Cathedral,* essentially Romanesque, offers surprises with art of our own era, by Marc Chagall, John Piper, and Graham Southerland. Not far from town are such splendid country houses as *Goodwood,* opulently eighteenth-century and exquisitely furnished in period; *Uppark,* classic in style, the home of Emma Hamilton before she became Lord Nelson's celebrated mistress, and art-filled; *Petworth,* with a baker's dozen paintings by Turner among much art; *Clandon Park,* a Rococo jewel with exceptional furniture, porcelain, and jade; *Arundel Castle,* derring-do medieval in look; and *Bateman's,* where author Rudyard Kipling lived with his family between 1902 and 1936.

Rye: That leaves little Rye, Sussex's time-stood-still town: an enchanting period piece with an easily walkable core, whose cobbled Mermaid Street has nary a modern appurtenance to mar its profile. A thirteenth-century tower houses the *Rye Museum,* and *Lamb House* is the Georgian mansion in which Henry James wrote *The Wings of the Dove* and *The Ambassadors.*

THE SOUTHWEST

BRISTOL

The city from which John and Sebastian Cabot sailed to the New World in 1497 and the very same that today globally exports the celebrated sherry that takes its name, Bristol—principal port, hub of commerce, and cultural seat of southwest England—deserves better acquaintance, especially in the case of visitors to its infinitely smaller but currently more celebrated neighbor, Bath (but a dozen miles distant and earlier recommended as a day-excursion point).

Badly bombed in World War II and with a core that might well have been more attractively rebuilt, Bristol—a metropolis of half a million—nonetheless brims with vitality and, upon occasion, beauty.

Built over a span of centuries, medieval through Victorian, *Bristol Cathedral* is one of the loveliest such of any in the big-city group. The *City Museum and Art Gallery* is big on French work—Delacroix and Courbet through the Impressionists, with Italians, Flemings, and the eighteenth-century English school well-represented, too. Two house-museums—*Georgian House* (eighteenth century) and *Red Lodge* (sixteenth century) are stunners—and the 702-foot-long suspension bridge over the Avon Gorge in suburban Clifton is an engineering marvel dating to 1829.

Nearby *Wells* is the seat of an exceptional cathedral, consecrated in 1239, with a spectacular West Front, a sublime Gothic interior, an adjacent and aged Bishop's Palace, and a nearby street, Vicar's Close, lined by fourteenth-century stone houses.

EXETER

Loveliest of the Devon towns, Exeter was settled by Romans, knew later Saxons, was awarded charters by no less than three medieval kings (John Richard I, and Henry II), was inhabited briefly by two later sovereigns (Charles I and Charles II), and was frequented by Elizabeth I's derring-do sea captains—Drake, Hawkins, and Raleigh. Its cathedral can be ranked with the great ones in the European spectrum, easily among a handful of Britain's finest, a Gothic beauty whose nave is one of the kingdom's monumental esthetic experiences, with its rib vaulting extending

300 unbroken feet. Take in the town's *Guildhall*, history-laden and treasure-crammed; have a look at the Reynolds' and other English paintings in the *Royal Albert Museum*, and at the hundred-plus boats in the town's old port, constituting the *Maritime Museum*.

Allow time, if you can, for a drive through *Dartmoor National Park*, a mix of quaint villages, trout-filled streams, and rugged mountains. Pay your respects to the *Mayflower's* passengers, at the Mayflower Stone in *Plymouth*, whose other draws are a pair of historic house-museums (Elizabethan and Merchant's) and the City Museum and Art Gallery. Stroll through coastal *Dartmouth*, noting seventeenth-century houses on Butterwalk, and the turn-of-century Royal Naval College complex; Kings Edward VIII and George VI were students, as was the current heir to the throne, Prince Charles. And consider inspection of distinguished country houses in the neighborhood, such as *Saltram, Buckland Abbey,* and *Ugbrooke*.

CORNWALL

Constituting England's southwest corner, Cornwall—rockbound, cliff-backed, cove-tucked, beach-bordered—is quite the most exotic of England's counties. Its ace-in-the-hole is *St. Ives*, which could win—not without fierce competition to be sure—the Cornwall Natural Beauty Sweepstakes. It is on the rocky—and more magnificent — north shore of the Cornwall peninsula, westerly enough to be close to landmark *Land's End* (Britain's westernmost point) and south shore towns like *Penzance* and *Falmouth*. Writers like D. H. Lawrence and Virginia Woolf were drawn to Cornwall, no less so than artists. Indeed, the home of the late sculptor Dame Barbara Hepworth is a memorial museum, with a generous collection of her work.

But St. Ives itself—descending a mountain to a jumble of narrow, commercial streets that front its central quay—

is a charmer to poke about in, and in summer, cruise boats depart its piers to nearby villages. *St. Michael's Mount* is a translation—not only in words, but physically as well— of Brittany's Mont Saint-Michel, a medieval castle perched atop a mini-mountain on a mini-island. *Tintagel* straddles a north coast cliff, still with remains of an ancient monastery and castle associated with the King Arthur legends. And *Truro*, Cornwall's chief town, is the seat of an impressive nineteenth-century Gothic-style cathedral, and the County Museum—with a particularly strong collection of English paintings, including Lely, Kneller, Hogarth, Gainsborough, and Constable.

THE MIDLANDS

NORWICH AND EAST ANGLIA

Norwich: The region's easternmost town of consequence, Norwich goes back a thousand years, is at once handsome and hilly, and boasts a pair of landmarks: a cathedral that is dominantly Romanesque and boasts a spectacular nave and cloister; and a castle whose construction spans many centuries and today operates as a regional historical museum. *Strangers Hall* shelters a score of seventeenth- and eighteenth-century-furnished rooms. There are three nearby country houses of distinction: *Sandringham House,* a royal family retreat built by Edward VII at the turn of the century; *Blicking Hall,* an outstanding seventeenth-century mansion; and *Holkham Hall,* designed by William Kent in the eighteenth century and with a 50-foot-high Marble Hall.

East Anglia: Though better known for his paintings of southerly Salisbury Cathedral, early nineteenth-century painter John Constable was born and bred in East Anglia —and painted it, as well. It's fun to come upon villages you'll recognize from his paintings in big-city museums, like *East Bergholt* (the hamlet where Constable was born), *Flatford, Stoke-by-Nayland,* and most especially, *Dedham,* whose landmark St. Mary's Church is a Gothic stunner. Two nearby towns, *Lavenham* (with still another ranking Gothic church and a superb Guildhall) and *Sudbury* (with the house, now a museum, where eighteenth-century painter Thomas Gainsborough was born and raised) are visit-worthy, too. And of the country houses in the neighborhood, the most unusual is *Ickworth* (just outside the pretty cathedral town of *Bury St. Edmunds*), an early nineteenth-century conceit that consists of a 500-foot-long rotunda whose center is taken up with a 104-foot-high dome, with curved wings on either side the setting for a series of elegant state rooms.

LINCOLN AND THE GREAT MIDLANDS HOUSES

The Romans dubbed it *Lindum,* with today's name a derivative. *Lincoln* is the city to which William the Conqueror sent deputies to build both castle and cathedral. If the former is more a case of fragments than a cohesive whole, the latter, *Lincoln Cathedral*—with its ravishingly sculpted West Front—is one of England's most beautiful. There are Turner paintings in *Usher Art Gallery* of early nineteenth-century Lincoln and the neighboring town of Stamford. *Belton House,* due south, is Baroque and with a portrait of King Edward VIII in the library (he was godfather of the landlord, Baron Brownlow).

But the region abounds in stately homes: *Newstead Abbey,* originally twelfth century and with a Byron Museum dedicated to memorabilia of the famous poet; *Kedleston Hall,* a masterwork of the eighteenth-century architect-designer Robert Adam; *Hardwick Hall,* the Tudor mansion called after the very same Bess of Hardwick whose third husband was custodian of the imprisoned

Mary Queen of Scots for 15 years; *Sudbury Hall*, a onetime royal residence (Dowager Queen Adelaide, widow of William IV, called it home for several years); *Burghley House*, whose builder was the first Lord Burghley, Elizabeth I's treasurer and which boasts a bed in which Elizabeth slept and a magnificent cache of Old Master paintings; *Althorp*, the originally sixteenth-century home of Earl Spencer, father of the Princess of Wales, whose husband is heir to the throne; and *Chatsworth*, arguably the most sumptuous of the lot—the splendid seat of the Duke and Duchess of Devonshire.

A WESTERLY CATHEDRAL TRIO

It is not in every region of Britain—or in any country in Europe, for that matter—that a trio of outstanding ancient cathedrals, each dominating a country town, is to be found within 15 to 20 miles of one another, and good friends, at that. The choirs of Worcester, Gloucester, and Hereford cathedrals collaborate in a unique annual music festival, each cathedral serving as the site of the performances every third August.

Worcester is at its prettiest in that part of the town flanking the bucolic banks of the River Severn and its cathedral. Of the riverbank cathedrals, it comes close to ranking with that of Durham. Look down the long nave, partly Norman but with Gothic embellishments. Take in the choir, the Lady Chapel, and the crypt, not failing to observe the tomb of Prince Arthur, elder brother of Henry VIII. If Arthur had lived to reign, England might still be a predominantly Catholic country.

Gloucester: The cathedral in Gloucester, largest of the trio of towns, was originally eleventh-century Romanesque and might still be, had its administrators, in the fourteenth century, not agreed to bury the body of the murdered King Edward II. The crush of pilgrims from all over Britain to the Royal tomb impelled rebuilding, so that Gloucester reemerged a monumental Perpendicular Gothic structure —one of the finest such extant—with a massive east window (38 by 72 feet) and unsurpassed fan vaulting in its cloister.

Hereford: That leaves lovely Hereford, a perky market town whose Gothic cathedral, edging the River Wye, is squat and squarish, dominated by a fourteenth-century tower, with its special treasures a clutch of chained books—early manuscripts chained in position to discourage theft—in its library.

THE NORTH

YORK AND YORKSHIRE

York: Surely the most romantic of the northern cities, York —named by the Romans (*Eboracum*)—was the seat of Saxon kings. It later became headquarters of the Archbishop of York, whose throne is in *York Minster,* largest of the English Gothic cathedrals, which staggers with its wide nave, enormous central tower, massive crypt, and matchless stained glass. *Treasurer's House,* the adjacent, onetime residence of cathedral treasurers, is handsomely furnished. A pair of venerable prisons now house the *Castle Museum;* the *Railway Museum* is No. 1 of its type in Britain; remnants of Roman York fill the *Yorkshire Museum;* and the *York Art Gallery* is a charmer.

The cathedral in not-far-distant *Ripon* runs an architectural gamut—Saxon, Romanesque, and Gothic. *Harrogate* is a pretty spa town, and of the region's country houses, two are super-standouts: *Harewood House,* the mid-eighteenth-century home of Lord Harewood—a first cousin of the Queen—designed in part by Robert Adam, and with art-filled state rooms; and *Castle Howard*, designed by the same Sir John Vanbrugh who created Blenheim Palace near Oxford, with a great central dome sheltering the 80-foot-high Great Hall, and contemporary eminence resulting from its having served as Brideshead, the country house in which much of the TV serialization of Evelyn Waugh's novel, *Brideshead Revisited*, took place.

A QUARTET OF NORTHERN CITIES

Birmingham, southernmost of this group, has four aces-in-the-hole: Old Masters, English greats, and French Impressionists in its *Museum & Art Gallery;* still more art treasures in its *Barber Institute of Fine Arts;* concerts by the noted *City of Birmingham Symphony* ("CBSO"); and performances at the "Rep," the noted *Birmingham Repertory Theatre.* From Birmingham, excursions are in order to contemporary *Coventry Cathedral* and the handsome, half-timbered towns of *Shrewsbury* and *Ludlow.*

Liverpool's lures are threefold: *Liverpool Cathedral*, which opened in 1978 and is the largest Anglican cathedral in the world—magnificently neo-Gothic; *Walker Art Gallery,* one of Britain's finest such; and the relatively recent *Merseyside Maritime Museum.* (Nearby *Chester,* with a Gothic cathedral, is one of England's more attractive smaller cities.)

Manchester, mercantile and undeservedly much maligned (to which British Airways flies nonstop from New York), has an underappreciated, architecturally distinctive Victorian-Edwardian core. It also has an underappreciated, mostly Gothic cathedral; the top-rank *Manchester City Art Gallery* (its Baroque-era Dutch works are standouts); and such nearby country houses of note as *Heaton Hall* and *Lyme Park.*

Newcastle—strategically situated on the River Tyne, where it flows into the North Sea—descends a hill to its busy waterfront. Its handsomest thoroughfare is Grey Street, the bend of which presents an array of facades dating to the early nineteenth century. The cathedral, with a crownlike tower, is fifteenth century and eye-filling; and the paintings are first-rate in *Laing Art Gallery.* There are four nearby points of interest: Roman-built *Hadrian's Wall,* going back 18 centuries; turreted, originally twelfth-century *Alnwick Castle,* opulently furnished; little *Washington Old Hall*—home to the ancestors of President George Washington as long ago as 1183, when it was built by the de Wessyngton family (the Anglo-Saxon spelling of Washington)—with Old Glory flying in the Great Hall; and *Durham Cathedral,* in the nearby town whose name it takes, edging the River Wear, and England's premier Romanesque church.

SCOTLAND

EDINBURGH AND GLASGOW

Scotland's Top Two cities are conveniently close to each other—train time is but 45 minutes between the two—and interestingly disparate.

Edinburgh, the capital, has four absolutely requisite destinations: *Edinburgh Castle,* on a rocky crag dominating the city, a medieval masterwork for long the seat of Scottish kings; *Palace of Holyrood House,* at once the Royal Family's Edinburgh headquarters (with visitable State Rooms) and the scene of the murder of Mary Queen of Scots' secretary, Rizzio, by courtiers with whom Mary's second husband, Lord Darnley, was collaborating; *St. Giles's Cathedral,* unusual squarish Gothic and history-rich; and the *National Gallery of Scotland*—with a major Scottish Painters section

(Raeburn, Ramsay, Wilkie) and fine English and Continental works, as well.

The nearby *Scottish Borders* area is excursion territory, its lures a clutch of country houses—Traquair House, Mellerstain, Floors Castle, and Bowhill especially.

Glasgow: Bigger, heavily mercantile-industrial Glasgow surprises first-time visitors with its gracious Victorian core. It pleases with its buildings, as well, by the turn-of-century Art Nouveau architect-designer Charles Rennie MacIntosh; its splendid Gothic cathedral; and a quartet of museums, which make it an all-Europe ranker of an art center: the relatively recently opened (and brilliant) *Burrell Collection;* the palatial *Glasgow Art Gallery and Museum;* the University of Glasgow's *Hunterian Art Gallery;* and eighteenth-century *Pollok House,* brimming with Spanish masterworks.

THE HIGHLANDS

The green and rolling Highlands hills extend north from their southern extremity in the neighborhood of *Perth* (an agreeable little town on the River Tay with adjacent Scone Palace its No. 1 attraction) to the westerly town of *Inverness* (not far from Colloden Battlefield, site of the decisive battle lost by the Jacobite army of Bonnie Prince Charlie in 1746; and Cawdor Castle, whose central tower went up in 1454) and to easterly *Aberdeen* (Britain's northernmost city of consequence, with a sleeper of an art museum, no less than three cathedrals, and such outlying stately homes as Haddo House, Crathes Castle, and Craigevar Castle, not to mention Balmoral Castle, the Royal Family's summer vacation venue.

Glamis Castle, where Elizabeth the Queen Mother and Princess Margaret were born, is the very same where Shakespeare set the murder of Duncan in *Macbeth. Blair*

Castle is the seat of the only private army allowed by law in the United Kingdom. And there are two lakes of note: *Loch Ness* (with the Loch Ness Monster Exhibition on its shore) and southerly *Loch Lomond*, just north of Glasgow.

WALES

Cardiff, capital of the 60-by-160-mile principality, is lively and friendly, and has four destinations of import: the *National Museum of Wales* (its range early Christian artifacts to regalia worn by Prince Charles at his investiture as Prince of Wales, and beyond, to Old Masters by the likes of Fra Angelico, Gainsborough, and fellow eighteenth-century English painters, and the French Impressionists); the *Welsh Folk Museum,* with representative buildings from all over Wales that have been moved to an 18-acre site adjacent to a fine Elizabethan castle; *Llandaff Cathedral,* essentially Gothic; and *Cardiff Castle,* originally medieval but with heavy nineteenth-century restoration.

Beyond the capital, concentrate on the ring of derring-do castles built by England's King Edward I to overawe the Welsh in the thirteenth century. *Caernarvon Castle,* where Princes of Wales are invested, is the most impressive; others include *Caerphilly, Carmarthen, Harlech,* and *Conwy.*

North Wales is the site of splendid country houses, like *Plas Newydd, Powys Castle, Chirk Castle,* and *Erddig;* and it boasts a pair of Britain's smallest Anglican cathedrals —*St. Asaph* and *Bangor.* And you don't want to miss *St. David's* (its bay is Wales's westernmost point), whose Gothic cathedral is among Britain's most atmospheric.

Acknowledgments

The pleasure of researching a book with the subject of this volume—London—has been considerably enhanced by the cooperation and counsel extended by Bedford Pace, skilled Public Relations Director of the British Tourist Authority in New York; his creative colleague, Lewis Roberts, BTA's North America Director of Marketing; and Robert Titley, Information Director at BTA; with all of whom I have been privileged to work, as well, in connection with this book's companion volume, *Britain at Its Best*, not to mention other assignments over a sustained period.

I am grateful, too, for the help of two longtime friends at British Tourist Authority's London headquarters, knowledgeable Press Facilities Officer Peter ffrench-Hodges and his astute associate, Catherine Althaus; no two Londoners know London better! Special appreciation, too, to Don Ford, BTA's North America chief, based in New York.

Max Drechsler, research editor for my books and a confirmed Anglophile like me, has been of immeasurable help; so has still another Anglophile, my agent—and a frequent visitor to London—Anita Diamant. I'm appreciative, too, of the support of the Big Three at National Textbook/Passport Books—S. William Pattis, Leonard I. Fiddle, and Mark R. Pattis; and my skilled and sympathetic editor, Michael Ross.

I want also to thank, alphabetically, the following friends and colleagues on both sides of the Atlantic, for their personal kindness and professional cooperation: Douglas Barrington, O.B.E.; Peter Bates, Willy Bauer, Georgia Beach, Doreen Boulding, Scott Calder, Mary

Carroll, Myrto Cutler, Judith Dagworthy, Richard Davis, Michael Duffy, Patrick Gaillard, Nicholas F. Gomez, Paul G. Grunder, Linda Gwinn, Nicola Hancock, Robert Heim, Peter Herbert, Judy Hoade, Mary Homi, Ronald F. Jones, John W. Lampl, Al Madocs, Irene Mann, Richard P. McGinnis, Wolfgang Nitschke, Ramón Pajares, William Pound, Sally Price, Kirk Ritchie, Robin Rue, Brigit Sapstead, Bob Schaeffer, Stefano Sebastiani, Giles Sheppard, Morris Silver, Nick Tarayan, Patricia B. Titley, John B. Waring, and F. Paul Weiss.

—R.S.K.

Index

.

About the Author

Robert S. Kane's initial writing stint was as editor of the [Boy Scout] *Troop Two Bugle* in his native Albany, New York. After graduation from Syracuse University's noted journalism school, he did graduate work at England's Southampton University, first making notes as he explored in the course of class field trips through the Hampshire countryside. Back in the United States, he worked, successively, for the *Great Bend* (Kansas) *Daily Tribune, Staten Island Advance, New York Herald Tribune,* and *New York World-Telegram & Sun* before becoming travel editor, first, of *Playbill* and, later, of *Cue* and *50 Plus* magazines; he writes regularly for *Travel & Leisure* and leading American and Canadian newspapers, and frequently discusses travel on TV and radio talk shows. *Africa A to Z* was the progenitor of his acclaimed 14-volume A to Z series, which in turn led to the creation of the current World at Its Best Travel Series. A past president of both the Society of American Travel Writers and the New York Travel Writers' Association, Kane makes his home on the Upper East Side of Manhattan.

DATE DUE

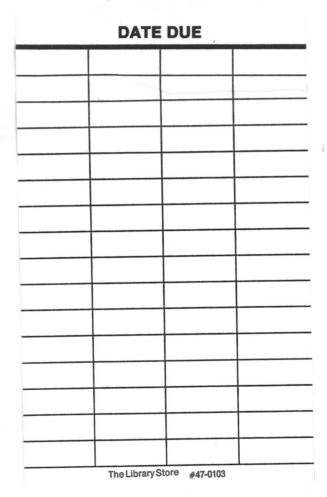